What People

Maya Mire

An extraordinary, fascinating story; well-written.
Anne Baring, author of *The Dream of the Cosmos: A Quest for the Soul*

Maya Mire

A Spiritual Journey into Cosmic Truth
and the Dawning of a New World

Maya Mire

A Spiritual Journey into Cosmic Truth
and the Dawning of a New World

Paul Nugent

6TH
BOOKS

London, UK
Washington, DC, USA

CollectiveInk

First published by Sixth Books, 2024
Sixth Books is an imprint of Collective Ink Ltd.,
Unit 11, Shepperton House, 89 Shepperton Road, London, N1 3DF
office@collectiveinkbooks.com
www.collectiveinkbooks.com
www.6th-books.com

For distributor details and how to order please visit the 'Ordering' section on our website.

Design: Lapiz Digital Services
Front cover: Indigo wall piece by Masao Kiyoe (private collection)

UK: Printed and bound by CPI Group (UK) Ltd, Croydon, CR0 4YY
Printed in North America by CPI GPS partners

We operate a distinctive and ethical publishing philosophy in all areas of our business, from our global network of authors to production and worldwide distribution.

Contents

The quotations and photographs in this book that were originally published by The Aetherius Society, and the photographs from The Aetherius Society's archives remain copyright to The Aetherius Society. Permission has been granted for their use by the International Directors of The Aetherius Society.

Disclaimer: The personal views expressed in this book are those of the author and are not necessarily those of The Aetherius Society.

Preface

This is an unusual story that in all probability breaks new mental ground. It will appeal to some but, almost certainly, not all.

Some readers will already know or have part of the story, albeit seen from varyingly different angles. In that sense it will be like the five blind persons each holding one part of the elephant and each believing that the part they are feeling, be it the tail, the trunk, the leg, the tusk or the ear, is the most accurate if not complete description of the animal.

That argument will inevitably be even more so when we are metaphorically blind people talking about a subject as vast as the history of ourselves, how we arrived here and where we are today. We each have different standpoints and our understandings will inevitably agree in part but doubtless there will come points of disagreement, some of which will be strongly held.

One thing we hopefully can all agree upon is that we are a world in crisis; or, as the bumper sticker says, "If you're not appalled you haven't been paying attention." A lot of us are paying attention and we are becoming increasingly alarmed for all kinds of reasons, most justifiably so; but it can lead to more heat than light being put out. And one of the last things we need is more heat.

The description of our predicament contained within these pages is one more perspective. Naturally, I believe it to be the most complete and compelling understanding of the overall picture and this will, for that reason, raise the dander on others' equally but differently held opinions. So be it. It is important, if not essential, to have the conversation so long as it is not while Rome endlessly burns. We need a solution and we need it rather fast.

With all that aside, while I presently hold the conch let me remind you all that nobody is forced or even required to read this book, though I hope you will. Nor is anyone asked to believe a word of what I have to say. What is important, and the very reason that I wrote the book, is that the message it contains has been profoundly true for myself. It has carved and shaped not just my adult life but even stems back into my earliest childhood memories. Indeed, I even go further than that in terming Part I, *The Things I Knew Before I Was Born*. As such, it has been important for me to now let these things out. They have been brewing.

Part I is a description of my own journey through life that brought me to my understanding: this intuitive sense of destiny that we all carry in perhaps the same way as the spermatozoa seek out the egg; or to put it a little less sensitively, how the pigeon finds its way home.

Part II tells what it is that I found. I began by calling this second and main part of the book *A Cosmic Vision for the New World* but later, while talking to myself out on my bicycle— which I do each morning, always to the sound of my own thoughts—I changed the word Vision for Scripture. I believe it to be so; and when we are talking about anything so holy, and which we consider to be so utterly true, then that is the term we must use. And most especially so when we believe it to be the most complete and concise understanding of something as sacred and profound as our collective, global predicament.

The story goes a long way back as you will read assuming you at least start, for the tale in that regard does commence at the beginning, almost literally. Although, in saying that, this Preface—which I was advised to write—is coming at the very end of all else that I have otherwise written.

Thank you for at least reading this far.

Introduction

We stand at the threshold of the greatest change in the total history of our evolution upon Earth.

It is comparable to the time when we emerged from waterborne creatures crawling through the mud and slime as amphibious beings into the discovery of land and sky, beyond our comprehension to fathom; and yet which has the feeling of coming home.

We are here at the start of something vast, and yet it is not imaginary. It is more our past that has been bound in unreality and fiction. It has been a lost time, precipitated by the fall of Maldek millions of years ago. The deep sleep of our collective inertia which followed is now ending, with a reemergence of our true being into the Garden of Eden before we fell.

It is a long story, and it is necessary for us to know it such that we can understand it, such that we can make it real. It is your story, and it is my story for it is our story—the human story; and in this human story it is necessary for us to look beyond ourselves to the skies and into the heavens such that we can believe the narrative and the wholeness of everything.

It is the timeless story encased in everything, and to be encased in everything is to be encased in Love. For Love is where it all began, and where it all shall be ended; and our time to know of it is now.

Part I:

The Things I Knew Before I Was Born

To tell the story of anything, you have to tell the story of everything.
Thomas Berry, Christian Cosmologist

There's only God's Time—which is NOW—and it's all happened anyway.
George King, Astro-Metaphysician

He who would true valour see, let him come hither.
John Bunyan, author of *The Pilgrim's Progress*

Dedicated to my parents,
Nicholas and Anne,
who kindly gave me birth.

Chapter 1

Early Years

It is difficult to know when it all began but a good place to start might be Maldek. It was, by all accounts, a very, very long time ago—over 18 million years—and it marks the point when, if nothing else, we shied away from the evolutionary path and fell into a very deep chasm of cosmic darkness. Time, as we knew it, ended. The consequences were not good. Sleep, to all intents and purposes, was better than being awake, or so it seemed.

Some might dispute this, and well they might. Up to a point the accuracy and details of Maldek are open to scrutiny and up for speculation. I prefer to accept the teaching of my Spiritual Master, George King, about whom and whose teachings this book is primarily about, for he understood these things and knew of them well. One might say, albeit tongue-in-cheek, that of this distant time and the darkness which sprang around it, "In the kingdom of the blind, the man with one eye is King."

My part in all this is minimal and only slightly less obscure, and brings me to contemplate the things I knew before I was born. It's an odd thing to consider by and large but I am being reminded of them with persistency; and, as much to the point I sense, as do many others, an Awakening—a stirring: a sense of a sleeping princess who has been found and kissed, and that the days of darkness and forgetting are drawing to a rapid end.

Even more to the point, I am here to argue that I knew the prince and of those who came with him; and if I know not of the princess I know of that which has been kissed and why, and it is perhaps my part to speak of it. Hence the remembrance of those things I knew before I was born. They are relevant and known by us all; to wit, not only is there incredible beauty within and throughout creation, but it is quite literally "That Which Is."

I regret this cliché, the mother of all clichés, but it is indisputable and unavoidable and I would be remiss not to include and account for it, first and foremost. For it is the backdrop to everything, even before Time and Space.

It is the one great thing we all knew before we were born — this Cosmic Sense of Infinite Being. There is no escaping it, and not only is there no escaping it, there is no accounting for it such that we are capable of, but there are those who are. This is the second thing I, and we all knew before we were born.

"Pay honour first to the Immortal Gods as Order hath established Their Choirs"; thus began *The Golden Verses* of the Pythagoreans who seemingly understood these things with a certain mathematical precision. Yes indeed, the choirs of Cosmic Hierarchy are ordered, choirs being a choice word of exactness. So these things are unescapable — they are Life and they are Breath, and this is, of course, another great cliché but nonetheless unavoidable. These are just two of the things we knew before we were born. They are not merely a part of the Grand Scheme, they are the Grand Scheme. And so it is. The case was never open nor ever closed. It merely is, and we are a part of it, and this is just the beginning.

The princess has been kissed in the tower and life in the castle — in the Kingdom of Earth — is stirring. I bow before you for, as I say, I knew the prince who entered this castle and of those who came with him, and it was my part, however small, to be there and now speak of it. It is just one more of those things I knew before I was born. And so it is.

Speaking of birth, such as it was, just before dawn on October 3rd, 1958, in the ancient university city of Cambridge, England, during one of the greatest karmic manipulations to take place in modern times, the only other comment I will note aside from the fact that I was pulled out by tongs having been stuck or confused in the womb, or else just reluctant to appear, I entered the hospital inside the womb of my mother on the day she found a four-leaved clover. I take it as a lucky sign for both of us.

Within a few months, six days before my Master climbed Kinder Scout in the Peak District of central England, and being the human instrument through whom this eighth and penultimate mountain in the British Isles became charged with spiritual power in the midst of another essential karmic aspect of this planetary awakening, I was christened, as it turned out, on St. Paul's day. My parents did not know. The name, not known in over thirty generations of Nugents, apparently seemed appropriate though it has taken me most of my life to become accustomed to it.

There is so much love to speak of, another great thing I knew before I was born, that early life and childhood led me to pleasure and ease, and much laughter. That an early nickname at boarding school—only miles from Holdstone Down, the first mountain to have been charged with spiritual power in July, 1958—was "Grin" summed up my overall nature and disposition. I loved the world and felt loved by it in return. Learning was secondary at best, and in the years which came to follow almost all my schoolboy study fell away as if tired and devoid of purpose, dead to the world.

I ended my school years empty-handed save for a handful of friends I retain to this day and a slight nagging sense, especially now, of opportunities missed. But the excuse I have carried all along is that I was never taught the only thing I wanted to know and more to the point none, save one, seemed capable of teaching it; nor did they even seem to know that it even was: that God Is, and that God Is All.

Such things were not taught in school however good that schooling was, at least for myself, and I left rather a lost and forlorn chap, my parents financially poorer and a world as I saw it less happy than the one I had sensed as a child. I was just seventeen.

My Master for almost all of that time had lived in America. I did not know he was even alive, unless I chose to reflect upon the things I knew from before I was born.

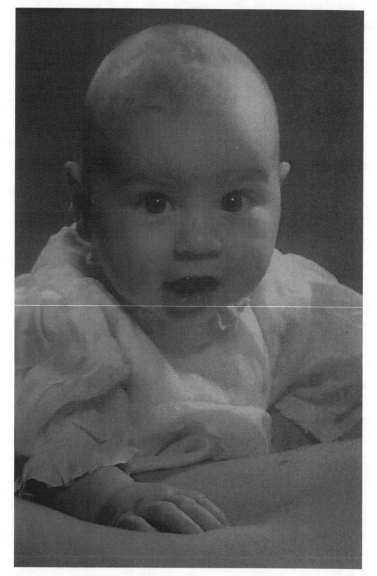

The author at his christening, January 25, 1959

Chapter 2

Finding My Feet

By this point in my life I was adrift in a small and rather unambitious harbor with little direction and no real inclination to head out to sea. As such, I went to the local college to reattempt some of the exams I had failed at private school. One year later, in the summer of 1977, I succeeded in obtaining the lowest passing grade in English literature and cashed it in at one of the few places which would even consider such academic paucity; finding myself studying Hotel Management in the southern coastal town of Bournemouth enticed there by a friend from school who had embarked on the same course the previous year.

Still a fish out of water, I had even less interest in hotels when I left three years later than when I had entered. However, in my final year it did introduce me to the subject of wine and at least I discovered a potential career that I could take sufficiently seriously. Perhaps more to the point, it had indirectly led me to my first unknowing encounter with The Aetherius Society, the organization I was later to join and which has gone on to become the fundamental purpose of my life, and the realization of one of three great incredible things I knew before I was born. Indeed, as a child of no more than ten or eleven, alone one day in the school library I knew my life would be lived as a life apart, within some form of institution and it coupled itself with a second innocent experience from those same childhood years when I felt a strong connection with Christ; an instinct that had come to me as I wandered alone upon a hillside in Yorkshire where my family lived at that time.

In the summer of 1979 as part of my college course, I spent many weeks in a butcher's shop on the Fulham Road in southwest London trussing poussins, small Cornish game hens, and although I had never come across these birds before felt much satisfaction preparing them, oblivious to the fact that my Master just a mile or two down the road would be ordering them with regularity. Each evening I would drive to the home at which I was staying past the very storefront that had housed the Society's headquarters in England since 1958. Little did I know it but I was already in the vicinity of the center of my future world.

Leaving hotels behind the following summer without either having entered one or carrying any intention of professionally doing so, I summoned whatever meager ambition I had to pursue a career in the wine trade, traveling to the south of France in October for the grape harvest with a large group of people I did not know. Loving the experience and even falling in love with a student from Oxford University, I went with at least some optimism and a slight skip in my step to the city of Bordeaux in search of further employment. Finding none though somewhat bolstered by the fact that I at least had an interview, I found myself back in England well before Christmas, by no means down and certainly not yet defeated.

Searching for work and a means to be in London, I secured a job without too much trouble working for a small independent chain of supermarkets and delicatessens. It wasn't exactly what I sought but it was better than any other offer I had or was likely to find; and, having emphasized my primary interest in wine, was informed that one of their two directors was a Master of Wine, that it was an important aspect of their business and that as a member of their management team I would be entered into a formal study of the subject.

Thus, in February, 1981, I was at last, however lowly, nonetheless on the rung of a so-called corporate ladder and, as much to the point, moving to London on a permanent basis sharing a room in southwest London with the very same friend who had enticed me to Bournemouth.

The wheels of my life, like for all of us, were turning by hook or by crook, displaying the wonderful truism from *Hamlet* that "There's a Divinity which shapes our ends, rough hew them how we will." Mine was pretty rough but things were shaping up, disguised though they were.

Chapter 3

A Spiritual Awakening

One indeed might well ask why I am writing all of this for it is, after all, a very ordinary story. Well, the answer to that is really quite simple. What took place, had taken place and indeed was taking place in part in the very local place of southwest London where I have just left off has forever changed our world in the most subtle yet profound way, and is the most fundamental explanation as to why our world is so dramatically changing; and will only continue to change and unfold with the coming years, culminating in a virtual utopian paradise not only that we all seek but, more essentially, we all knew to exist before we were born.

Speaking again of birth, I am reminded of the wonderful Buddhist story regarding the chances of birth being comparable to a one-eyed turtle randomly surfacing on a great ocean through the floating yolk of an ox. Of course the chance of such a thing is beyond calculation save to say the Tibetans consider it the same likelihood as being born.

Believe it or not, I agree with them and not only that, admire them for their veritable insight and imagery. It is a reality we have carelessly let go, and our forsaken world, described so well again in *Hamlet* as "an unweeded garden that grows to seed," is the inevitable result.

To be reminded of the supremacy of birth: the touchstone — nay, gemstone — of it; the uniqueness, the purity, the audacity, the essential primordial goodness of such a miraculous thing dispelling virtually all other forms of magic, is the primary purpose of us all. And so it is.

Returning to my tale, and what a tale it is, humanity interacted with the Cosmic Hierarchy from other worlds in the latter half

14

of the twentieth century and, as the flowering of these changes begins to manifest, it is necessary for those few of us, I among them who have been made aware of this cosmic pollination, to now speak of it; and in such a way that, hopefully, may be understood in order to be believed. For despite all of the odds, it is true!

My ordinary story, in part, is as ordinary as most others living on our planet and yet it allows me to introduce, or perhaps reintroduce, a preexisting knowledge that we all have and allow this to air itself more abundantly so that not only can the changes better manifest, but that we can also better understand them: To experience God in a most personal way and again, in that realization, to experience a sense of the Divine Love which exists within and surrounds us all.

I remained with that London firm for the following nine years, progressing to just short of becoming a Master of Wine under the tremendous influence and tutelage of my employer, Nicolas Belfrage, one of the few Masters of Wine at the time and one of the world's leading authorities in Italian wines. In 1983, I transferred within the company to become his assistant, helping to develop the subsidiary firm he had recently founded, Winecellars, which, four years later and despite its limited resources became, quite remarkably, *The Sunday Telegraph* "Wine Merchant of the Year" in Britain's first such challenge of its vintners.

I am essentially unaccustomed to winning awards and prizes, the only previous ones holding little to be proud of. At boarding school where I had failed almost all of my exams, I had become—indeed quite distinguished myself—the president of the illicit house drinking club celebrated with an ancient English pub sign known as the "Boozy Boar's Head," a pewter tankard engraved with the names of all previous presidents and the right to confer "colors," both full and half on all those whom I felt had distinguished themselves in the ancient art of froth blowing during my tenure. This, and the captaincy of water pistol shooting, was the only accolade I earned after ten years of academia at much personal cost to my long-suffering parents.

Aside from these, I had, in 1980, somewhat more to my credit been presented with the Stag Hunters' cup in the Somerset village of Porlock on the edge of Exmoor after winning a rodeo contest, defeating professional steeplechase jockey and winner of over 400 races, Richard Pitman, into second place. I had not been on a horse or pony since my earliest years of childhood.

However, by the time this latest accolade came around I had already undergone a most significant transition sensing shortly after joining Nick as his assistant, if not even a little before, something profoundly missing in my life. Unsure what it was and finding no such thing within my circle of friends, I became increasingly isolated and began, in my quest, to read the Bible unsure of where else to turn. Whatever was on the surface of my life began to be pushed aside as this deeply planted seed exerted its force and power, no less alarming to myself than those around me.

Both I and my world began to change in an unstoppable way and it was an unleashing of being through a secondary birth that combined awkwardness with innocence. I, like any of us, hadn't really seen it coming unless, of course, I chose to reflect upon the things I knew to be so from before I was born. My end, if not more precisely my spiritual beginning, was being shaped by Divinity's hand and there was nothing to do but look on. And so it was.

The Bible reading led, to be more precise, to a thorough and continuous reading of the four Gospels and to this day I retain the copy awarded to myself on July 14th, 1968, for obligatory attendance of "Crusader classes" at my Christian-based prep school, in which I had now begun to underline verses in the columns of its pages. I was not quite a recluse but I was changed, and in my changing began to attend Sunday evensong at Westminster Abbey in central London, not knowing of or being inclined towards any other more local church.

This forceful period in my life coincided with a discovery both of life and of London. I indulged myself in museums, art galleries, the theatre, music, and the stoic beauty of the city, as well as passing time in the public galleries of both the House of Commons and Lords where I learned to understand and applaud the process and ancient principles of democracy; yet I also observed that politics was limited to the perfection of second best, something never ultimately able to provide the solution to society's woes.

This solution was more spiritual in nature, remarkably summed up I thought at the time by Margaret Thatcher during a Cold War visit to the Soviet Union where she announced in a most visionary fashion, "I have indeed seen for myself that the road does indeed lead to the church." It epitomized the new direction of my own life, enunciated again to my ears by Alexander Solzhenitsyn in an article for *The London Times* in May, 1984, in which he wrote that the West "had lost its consciousness of God."

As such, I began to wax philosophical about almost everything discovering a love of Shakespeare who, I learned, was feasibly an ancestor, William Nugent; an Anglo-Irish nobleman born in 1550 as detailed in the book, *The Green Cockatrice* by Basil Iske. In the spring of 1984 I visited the author, who turned out to be a woman named Elizabeth Hickey, in her old castle in the village of Skryne in County Meath. As a local historian, she directed me to derelict Norman castles either built or inhabited by my Nugent ancestors together with the less derelict homes of distant cousins still favored to be living in the old country; my own line of forebears having been evicted as Catholics following the Battle of the Boyne in 1690, and resettled in the English colony of Antigua in the West Indies. An account of this blessed visit to Ireland made upon my moped was recorded in a poem I wrote at the time while resting one extremely wet afternoon in Connemara.

Life was, at this time, rich for me and intense. I reveled in it and in all the very healthiest ways of youthfulness, even joining Richmond Football Club where I trained once or twice a week and even managed to be included one Saturday afternoon as a reserve for the lowliest team in the club. The practice kept me reasonably fit and again introduced me to an entirely different arena of friends.

But it was the spiritual journey that both compelled and propelled me, taking its next direction into the study of Eastern philosophy at a school in London attended by Nicolas Belfrage, my spiritually-inclined employer. Here I learned of new remarkable things, at least to myself at the time, of Karma and Reincarnation—stunning concepts ancient beyond Christianity and as mysterious as a journey through the looking glass. Yet what resounded was an overwhelming essence of truth and profundity, both equal to their antiquity of thought. It was rigidly true and I began to wonder, as it grew against my new Christian roots, what the disciples and Apostles of Christ were doing now? Even more to the point what was Christ doing now? Where was Christ? Surely, as surprisingly voiced by Mrs. Thatcher, our most misguided world, lost even then, needed his spirituality, his realization, and his fundamental and absolute voice of truth. The pages of my own life were being turned. Indeed, had life actually come to life, and this was just the beginning.

I stayed with this school of philosophy for the next four years and would have stayed longer but by this time another spiritual seed had taken root that embraced and drew together my love of Christ and his teachings, the profundity of Eastern mysticism, and, equally importantly, the New Age concepts that were incorporated and manifested at the spiritual community of Findhorn in the north of Scotland which I attended in the summer of 1985 and experienced again the following year.

This introduction, and that of this all enjoining cornerstone, The Aetherius Society with its European headquarters just blocks away from where I now both lived and worked, had come about through Nick's part-time secretary, a woman called Patricia who had joined Winecellars shortly after myself. Prior to Pat's arrival another most comely woman had been employed but, much to my surprise and disappointment at the time, her typing inadequacies were too heavily flawed for Nick to retain her. Pat took her place and I have ever since come to see her and Nick as indispensable godparents in my own spiritual development at a time when I most especially needed them.

More than 30 years later, while drinking tea with Pat in a London café, she told me the strange story of how she had felt compelled to apply for that job despite its stipulation that applicants must have an interest in wine. As a teetotaler, she had none at all. Working above one of the company's own delicatessens, the three of us frequently indulged in memorable and somewhat extensive lunches in which various wines were inevitably sampled but more especially, spiritual and metaphysical discourses were held at length.

My formative years were now being solidified as I established a regular weekly routine that included philosophical study and work practices, rugby training, and on Sundays, attendance at The Aetherius Society in the mornings, invariably Speakers' Corner in Hyde Park or else some art gallery in the afternoon; and evensong at St. Martin-in-the-Fields in Trafalgar Square which in all likelihood I had helped to clean the night before as part of the church's "Scrub Club." Sunday evenings were, with luck and a fair breeze, rounded off with dinner in the apartment of two old and dear friends from school overlooking Clapham Common.

My transition to St. Martin's from Westminster Abbey had taken place sometime before when one Sunday afternoon, having time on my hands, I had wandered down Whitehall and entered the church finding it very much to my liking and with a greater sense of intimacy. Later, as I became something of a regular, I volunteered for the Scrub Club which consisted of a few somewhat lonely pensioners and one or two haphazard and slightly wayward souls, one of whom had wandered off into the Sahara Desert in search of God and was found dead on Easter Sunday.

The group was run by an elderly spinster who remarkably enough had known my father's family in Yorkshire many years before, and I sensed she had held an affection for my uncle Paddy who was killed in the Second World War. Moreover, she still retained a very long-standing friendship with a cousin of my father's even at the time I knew her which continued into their late 90s. Indeed, I became fondly attached to the Scrub Club joining them for day-outings and once hosting them all to lunch together with the legendary vicar of the church, Rev. Austen Williams. It was a deeply memorable lunch, in stark contrast to the normal dinner parties I had enjoyed with friends over the years, being made up of a strange mixture of folk unfamiliar with such invitations and yet with a warm and soulful undercurrent of human kindness.

Occasionally I would invite a number of friends to help give the old church a thoroughly good clean. It was used throughout the week as a shelter for many of London's homeless people and I will never forget one friend, whom I had met at the school of philosophy and who remains a beloved friend to this day, commenting afterwards that it was "more like sweeping up after a football match than dusting a few pews" as he had expected!

What began to emerge during this whole period in which I had found my fundamental reason for being, and which so definitely answered the vacancy I had experienced in my life just a few years before, was my association with The Aetherius Society. My weekly routine had now incorporated on a very regular basis attendance at the Society for their divine service on Sunday mornings.

What especially attracted me was the sense that here was a group of people of all ages, backgrounds and even nationalities, who had sought and found the same thing I was fundamentally seeking and for the same reason; and they had encountered something of outstanding and even unique value to the world which was living within them.

Most essentially, they epitomized the ancient proverb: *The fox knows many things but the hedgehog knows one big thing*. These people, although not especially worldly-wise, all undoubtedly knew one Big Thing, and yet it wasn't secretive and by no manner of means was it sinister. Indeed, quite the reverse. It had a spiritual intensity and an awareness that I had found more or less completely lacking elsewhere. These people had truly found something, a jewel; and not only did they deeply prize and cherish it, they understood it and used it in a remarkable and unique way in service to the world. As such, I always felt a sense of magic, a living magic in a *Lord of the Rings* kind of way when I attended and it adhered to me deeply; and, as if falling in love, I knew it had taken hold of me. It was, as I see it now, something I had known before I was born, like the premonition I had had as a child in the school library so many years before.

Life had become important, very important. Everything was important, and as I say, life had become alive. It was found, it was; it is!

The European headquarters in London in the 1980s

Chapter 4

The Aetherius Society

At the very heart and center of The Aetherius Society was its founder and president, a man recognized by its members as a Master, their Master; a new experience and concept to myself at the time. Only rarely did he visit the United Kingdom despite his English origin, being primarily resident in Hollywood, California, as good as a million miles away. Moreover, not only was there a tremendous mystique and aura surrounding him, there was a hierarchy among his followers that left me at the back of the crowd. There were those who knew him somewhat, those who had had a direct experience and contact with him if not numerous experiences, and those few at the very top of the organization who still had dealings with him.

It was a rich and heady mixture, compounded in its mystery by a simplicity of surroundings and a profound sense of the occult. For example, the temple was a small basement hall entered by narrow stairs at the top of which was a provoking old wooden carving of the three monkeys, "See no evil, hear no evil, speak no evil." As one descended members would already be seated in silent meditation, sitting in tight rows and often wearing a colored robe to signify their degree of initiation within the order. Incense burned and at the very front of the hall was a magnificent cross adorned with nineteen polished stones like jewels, each slightly different; and at the top of which was a golden symbol of the Sanskrit A-U-M combined together with a triangle forming the logo of the organization which, I was told, signified "God manifesting Itself through Wisdom."

Beside this cross, which was illumined by a bright magenta light bringing out its presence all the more, was a sign which read: *As you are on this planet, what you are on this planet, while you are on this planet, five Beings fight for your privilege to be so...* Whatever that was about I hadn't a clue but all of this mystery was intrinsically balanced by the essential spiritual goodness of the individuals who attended. Intoxicating was perhaps the simplest and best way to describe it all.

As the service began, the minister would descend the same steps into the dimly lit hall with a taper to light candles on the altar. The members who sat with a deep sense of seriousness and solemn purpose meanwhile joined in the recitation of mantra. The minister would then open the service in the small, cramped basement with mystical visualization practices, utterly foreign to the orthodoxy of the Christian church into which I had been raised and refound, and indeed would be visiting later that same day.

If I was not already in a slight swoon, I very soon would be. What transfixed me, utterly, in those early years and rooted me to my chair; what I knew would keep me coming back for more, what I knew was also so above this world and yet of the uttermost priceless value was the Voice of Jesus as if spoken live—the great living, still living, never dead Master Jesus as he spoke, and had indeed spoken in that very same hall through this unknown man and Master, George King, in the very year of my birth, 1958.

The words were pure, the voice was clear and it carried the absolute, complete unvarnished hallmark of simplicity and truth that was, in its way, shocking. And yet at the same time, it needed to be shocking. Our whole world is crying out for shock, not to scare us but to awaken. Shock speaks to us at a primal level beyond life and death, to the very nature of truth and the core of our being. And this is how Jesus sounded, at least to myself: strong, vital, unafraid; true. And at the same time it carried a message so anciently wise and yet equally new and profound, utterly mind-shattering, that I could only accept it for precisely what it was: the very crux of truth that in its way would silence even the greatest amongst us, bringing us all, should we know it, to our knees. We are nothing in the sight of it and in the sight of the Master who not only had lived among us but who, 2,000 years ago, we murdered; and who rose again to prove to us all one of the greatest truths in all our terrestrial existence.

It was a riveting experience each Sunday morning that I found deeply cleansing in the purest of earthly waters. I simply couldn't ignore it, and I knew I had discovered one of the essential milestones in my life that I had known to be so from before I was born. And so I braced myself for more. I took to it. I moved beyond being a stranger in their midst, even though I dared not at this stage plunge myself in too deeply with anyone. I would, in time, come to know each and every one in a baptismal sense, bathing myself in the same spiritual water.

It is hard to recollect these things entirely but as best as I recall my habit and routine stayed much the same for at least a year. Sunday afternoons still took in Speakers' Corner in Hyde Park where I admired the Methodist preacher, Lord Soper for his commitment to his own cause and his ability to always draw a crowd; or else I would visit a museum or otherwise go for a long walk, commonly in Richmond Park which I had come to know in all its various corners. The evening would still take in St. Martin's followed by dinner with Mike and Richard. I traveled everywhere on my red Honda moped called "Monty" and when it rained I clad myself in scarlet protective clothing that made me look like a tomato, as once described by the sister of a much loved girlfriend.

During the week I worked with wine, helping this small chain of supermarkets and delicatessens climb its way to becoming Wine Merchant of the Year through Nick's fine palate and my due diligence in other ways. It was all a time, I suppose, when my youth finally took form. I was not so much sure of myself as I was sure of where I was going even though I could not see and did not look much beyond my next experience at The Aetherius Society. Here I had found home. I knew it and believe those who were already there knew it too. All that remained was the chance to meet Dr. King, to stand before him; to experience directly for myself who he really was.

This opportunity finally, and yet firstly, presented itself on a mountaintop in the county of Devonshire in southwest England in 1985. It was July the Eighth, the most significant day in The Aetherius Society calendar. Though still not a member I had joined two coaches that departed the London headquarters at midnight and which would drive through the night to this mysterious location known as Holdstone Down overlooking the north Devonshire coastline in pristine English countryside, not far from where I had spent so much of my childhood.

We arrived not long after dawn in the village of Combe Martin with strong ties to the ancient myth of Jesus visiting this part of England. The official gathering on the mountain, referred to as a pilgrimage, would not start until 11:00 a.m. so I had time to take a swim in the cold refreshing water of the Bristol Channel, delighting in the charm of this sacred baptismal ritual and seeing the moon still shining high above in the bright morning sky.

Breakfast was taken in one of the several cafés nestled around the small harbor and though accompanied all the while by Pat, I felt shy and awkward as I was greeted by these fellow pilgrims, many of whom I had never seen before. The "elite," so to speak, were already gathered with Dr. King in a small home known as "The Retreat" that had been purchased in the village two years before. There was no chance of looking in or being seen to do so. There was a proverbial ladder to reach Dr. King and a long line of people ahead of me to climb it. If anything, being as I was a nonmember of the organization, at the very bottom of the ladder even among those waiting in line for the chance to climb it. So there you go.

There were about 200 people on the mountain that day who had traveled from all over the country. We gathered in a large circle with two or three ministers at its center being led by the priest, Richard Lawrence, whom I had come to know and regard as someone who, most like myself, had drunk deeply of the spiritual cup and was favored as the European Secretary to have close dealings with Dr. King.

Although only a few years older than myself, I looked up to him and admired him greatly. The other ministers walked in a long slow circle reciting mantra through loudhailers, keeping the rhythm in which we all joined. Into this circle were taken three, four, or six prayer team members each of whom not only knew by heart the blessings and prayers as given by Jesus in the ritual I had found so compelling but could deliver them with an intensity of power and feeling. This ritual continued for several hours with short breaks between each prayer session, often resulting in a change of mantra.

Of course, the additional buzz for everyone was the presence of Dr. King whom very few of the members had yet seen since his arrival from America only ten days beforehand. He came on to the mountain escorted by a handful of close followers and was keeping to one side of the hilltop. Eventually he came to join us, walking around and inside the circle. I, like everyone, was anxious to observe him but equally, was careful not to be seen to stare or even redirecting my main focus of intent which was the recitation of the mantra.

Gradually he worked his way around to where I was standing and then, about one yard away, he stopped and stared directly ahead of myself, never once from what I could tell looking in my direction. I cannot say why he stopped or what his thoughts were but it was my first encounter with my Master which, although I would never have known at the time, was the beginning of what would later become a surprisingly close relationship. The mountain, too, was to have profound implication for my mother at the exact time of Dr. King's passing almost twelve years later.

The following summer we returned to Holdstone Down for a repeat of 1985 except without Dr. King. However, what I recall especially was the sad feeling that I would never return to Devonshire in the same way as I had known and loved the county in my childhood for I had been changed by my new experiences. This disturbing thought caused me to disappear from the crowd when we stopped on the motorway for a meal-break during the journey back to London and I wandered off down what became a country lane, only to find a remote church into which I was able to enter. There I sat alone for several minutes questioning myself and this future direction which was increasingly showing itself ahead of me, but which in turn meant leaving behind so much of my far more familiar past. Staring at the cross upon the altar I received the strong impression that I must stay with this newly-found path and not be afraid of where it might lead. It was an important and encouraging moment and I ran back to the parked coaches, relieved to find the rest of the party still eating and seemingly unaware of my absence.

With this confirmation, perhaps seen in a more subtle way as a challenging fork in the road, I prepared myself to join The Aetherius Society eschewing the lesser level of Associate Membership in favor of Full, gently encouraged all the while by Pat. On September 26th of that year my membership was accepted.

I, meanwhile, had left London for Italy to stay in a rented farmhouse in Tuscany which I had organized together with two close friends, Mike and Chris, with whom I shared a house in Wandsworth and that Mike and I jointly owned. Six of us drove down in two cars, one of which carried on the roof a giant wicker laundry basket I had acquired from school to be used as a hamper for picnics. In Pisa we picked up two more friends, later to be joined in the Tuscan village by another old friend, Gavin, who was driving independently of us all with his new girlfriend. When he arrived in an even newer Porsche we needed no explanation as to why he had chosen not to be part of our convoy!

It was there, in the midst of such a memorable and happy vacation that, on October 3rd, I celebrated my twenty-eighth birthday. Lying in the long grass beneath the clear night sky, the only recognition I could say I had achieved was that I had become a member of The Aetherius Society. It was a consideration far from that idyllic Tuscan farmhouse and the company of my closest friends, but it was deep within my heart in a somewhat lonely place; yet in my soul I knew it the right place to be, however unbearable it would become to gradually loose myself from this deeply and dearly loved group of friends. It was, if I might be permitted for saying so, just something I had known from before I was born. And so it was.

A pilgrimage to Holdstone Down in Devonshire on July 8, 1985, where the author first saw Dr. George King

Chapter 5

Joining the Staff

Earlier in 1986, I had taken an eight-week course in mystical yogic practices utilized by members of The Aetherius Society, based in large part upon Dr. King's own spiritual practice that had led to his illumination more than 30 years before. Suffice to say, I adopted these exercises into my own daily life with such vigor that during one particular breathing practice I temporarily lost consciousness and fell flat on the floor with such velocity that I cut open my eyelid, requiring stitches. It was complicated to explain exactly to the doctor how this had happened. All the ancient mystery schools would have been centered on such breathing exercises, referred to as pranayama, as well as mantra and visualization techniques.

Such a daily regimen as I adopted inevitably led me to being at slight odds with Mike and Chris to whom such morning practices were strange and difficult to understand. Besides, they both had burgeoning careers, Mike as a city lawyer and Chris as a chiropractor working for a Harley Street doctor. My life was at variance with theirs, and although the friendships were deep and remain intact to this day, it was necessary, at least for myself, to move out.

At some point in 1987 I consequently took up residence in a small, rather gloomy apartment in Treport Street, southwest London, with The Aetherius Society taking up an increasing amount of my time. With membership had come more tangible friendships with others within this organization and I became increasingly torn away from my old way of life. Attendance at St. Martin's dried up. I even ended my study at the school of philosophy I had frequented for the past four years and, finally, selecting to attend an activity of The Aetherius Society on

Thursday evenings, I ended an important element in my study towards becoming a Master of Wine.

It was all as if the ground beneath my feet was shifting like the disintegration of an ice-shelf. I had made my choice however hard and potentially far harder for my parents and friends; but I was on the square I needed to be even though it was a long and silent farewell to all the early years of my life and an unknowingness, except in the deepest recesses of my soul, of what was to come. Little did I know it but I was even soon to leave England. The Divinity shaping our ends must occasionally cut deep to shape them accordingly.

Why was I doing this? What was it that was driving me so intently? Why couldn't I live a more balanced life? These were questions asked by others rather than by me of myself. My early apprenticeship was over. Though still young, I had come of spiritual age. The future and the future of my life were both awaiting; and all that I had so far learned, and most especially learned of The Aetherius Society and of the great living Masters who lay beyond this organization, was far too great and compelling to try and ignore. I knew it to exist and I knew it to be more meaningful than I would ever find elsewhere.

The path to truth is lonely, long and hard like each step of a thousand miles, but given the two choices, turning back would have been far harder; and what was more, what was the point? There was no point. This pilgrim was making his progress towards a Master he still hadn't formally met.

The motto of The Aetherius Society, taken from a transmission given by a Master from Mars through Dr. King in 1961 is, "Service is the Jewel in the Rock of Attainment," and it epitomizes their own creed. Inevitably, the amount of service any one person can give differs from another. The most committed members of the organization, as far back as the 1950s, had given almost all of their spare time to the work of Dr. King and the Society forming the staff; and in October, 1988, I took this step having gradually increased the amount of time I spent at the headquarters in London over the previous two years. The first year is spent as a trainee to determine whether the path and the student are suitable for one another. I still saw my old friends but far less frequently. There was never any actual rift; I had always done my best to fully explain myself but perhaps they secretly hoped this new way of life wouldn't last.

Then, in early 1989, Dr. King fell ill and the sounding word in England was that he may not live for very much longer. I found this especially alarming since I was one of the few, if not the only staff member in the world who had yet to actually meet his Master. As such, Richard Lawrence was advising us, should we wish to see our Master one more time, perhaps the last, to travel to America since, as indeed was the case, he was unlikely ever to return to the UK.

I was among the first to apply and on May 6th, 1989, left Heathrow bound for Los Angeles for a three-week period accompanied by a fellow staff member, Pete Higginson; someone I barely knew but a nicer companion I could not have had.

Fortune is indeed a funny thing but opportunities taken at their full can indeed lead one further than one might have otherwise dreamed. Landing in the warm afternoon sunshine of Los Angeles much later that same day, we were met by an icon of Aetherius Society history, Charles Abrahamson, in his large station wagon. Though I did not recognize him, Charles after greeting Pete looked at me with a smile, remarking that I was, "an unknown quantity!" Dr. King, we learned, was not currently at the headquarters in Hollywood but at his private home in Santa Barbara 100 miles to the north, being expected to return in a few days' time.

In terms of depth of experience within The Aetherius Society, Los Angeles was the deep end of the pool with staff members such as Charles having been at our Master's side virtually since his arrival in the United States in 1959. Though it is a cliché to say so, I could not have found myself among nicer people who were all too unaccustomed to meeting their fellow staff from England. I was more than greeted by friends, I was accepted as kindred at the very heart of the organization still in the time of its living master; a Master I was surely about to meet.

It is perhaps difficult for the reader to fathom and understand why, to the full extent that I did, I should have so detached myself from a loving family, friends, a promising career and even my orthodox Christian faith to follow this remote group of people which, on the face of it, resembled a suspicious cult believing in UFOs and advanced life beyond this planet. Why would I do this? What is the logical and emotional reasoning behind it, and can such really be justified? Is it not, as some thought at the time, throwing my life away in the guise of religious fanaticism? The truth is, I can and always have been able to answer those questions, never losing my faith or the deeper understanding of why I did what I did.

To be reminded of the Tibetan analogy of life being as utterly remarkable, unique even, as the one-eyed turtle surfacing upon a vast ocean through the floating yoke of an ox, I accept birth as a profound gift from God, summarized in the lines of a poem I wrote during the time of my great initial soul search:

And what have I done with birth?
It gave itself to me and with its gesture
I have sourly melted into shame, and guilt,
And aspirations to be great,
And all before the age of twenty-three.

Since that time I had come to marvel at life—the beauty of it, the reality of it, the graciousness of it, the purity and goodness of it; and as I say, even from earliest childhood and especially through my school days there was never any actual recognition of this, no celebration of it. And the consequences of all this ignorance or denial was a world embroiled in war, wealth and poverty, cruelty and crime; and in such a way as to threaten the very health of the planet. All these things profoundly moved me, affected me, and so disturbed me that I had to not only find an answer that could satisfy the clamoring of my own soul but also sufficiently ease my conscience to do something about it.

Discovering the life of Jesus in the New Testament was the first massive step in answering these questions but it didn't resolve what Jesus is doing today, nor equally, what is being done today; and when I encountered The Aetherius Society, however isolated it stood like a strange and remote island, it bore all the hallmarks of a brave, undaunted truth and action that I sought. It was infinitely more compelling than all the other aspects of my life no matter how pleasant they were and how well loved and supported I was.

Two vivid experiences in those formative years stand out. The first was one of those semiconscious dreams that one occasionally has shortly before waking. It was Sunday, March 9th, 1986, and as I lay in my bed I sensed the presence of an extraterrestrial intelligence: a tall, golden figure hovering to my side. And behind him I could see a picture of the planet from which he had presumably come—a radiant planet where there were fields of wheat that stood incredibly high, again with the same golden luster, and I mentally expressed my wish to go to where he had come from. And in hearing my plea the answer given back was, "You serve to leave... You serve to leave... You serve to leave." It was repeated over and over again like a mantra until I understood. One cannot just go because one wants to, one must serve. Serve one's world, serve one's fellow man; to love them as Jesus had himself loved and taught. It was a powerful moment that only drove me deeper into The Aetherius Society and I painted the letters "You serve to leave" together with the date in gold ink onto a large framed portrait of Christ that hung at the head of my bed.

A second experience came as I sat alone in the basement hall of The Aetherius Society in the Fulham Road the following year. An artist's impression of the Logos of Earth as visited by Dr. King in a projected state several years before had been unveiled during the Sunday service earlier that day, only I had been unable to attend due to my work at Winecellars. When I came to the Society that evening Richard Lawrence thoughtfully invited me to spend a few minutes in front of the painting alone. As I did so, the holy cross on the altar illumined in magenta to my side, I was very much drawn into the life-like painting becoming uniquely aware of the living reality of this flame with its energy, its power, its absolute divinity, and its great relevance to us all upon Earth.

And then, as I came out of this reverie, I heard laughter coming from the upper room where several staff members were gathered and I sensed in that moment the true spirit of brotherhood and sacrificial commitment they had each made in their lives, and their spiritual conviction of these cosmic teachings. And I intuitively knew that if I was unable to beat them by any other cause or means I must join them: the disciples of a New Age in a new calling yet profoundly good, and in recognition of a Master now living among us. It was a turning point from which I was never to look back.

Painting The Retreat in Combe Martin, Devonshire, in 1987

Chapter 6

Meeting My Master

A few days after Pete and I had arrived at the American headquarters, the Master left his home in Santa Barbara driven by his aide, Brian Keneipp, with the other full-time assistant, Richard Medway, arriving a few hours later having closed up the house and loaded the Master's personal items into the Society's pick-up vehicle.

Pete and I anxiously waited in the parking lot for the silver-gray Buick to pull in. I think we both felt caught in the difficult position of not knowing whether to step forward or stand back when the Master alighted from his car. Consequently we hovered somewhere between the two with the Master giving us a faint wave of acknowledgement. Evidently he knew we were here and somewhat expected. Later, word reached us that in the upcoming days he would be taking us on a "grand tour" of the property which naturally meant that no one else should be showing us around.

The American headquarters on Afton Place in Hollywood was purchased by the Society in 1965 and, at that time, comprised of the original temple with two adjacent bungalows. One was used for Dr. King's personal accommodation with a bedroom and bathroom at the rear for his main assistant, Monique Noppe; and the other bungalow, always referred to as "the Third," serving as a communal dining room and accommodation for some of the other staff with several additional out-buildings including a workshop.

Later, in the early 1970s, the neighboring bungalow was purchased being referred to equally as either "the Fourth" or "the Annex." The building has had several incarnations over the years but, when we arrived in 1989, it was primarily office space with accommodation for a resident staff member, Brian, at the time; and it has remained that way ever since.

Besides Charles Abrahamson, two other iconic figures in the history of The Aetherius Society were Dr. King's wife, Lady Monique, and her twin sister, Irène Noppe. Active Rosicrucians, the Noppe sisters first encountered the Master at a UFO convention in Los Angeles in July, 1959. Dr. King was accompanied by Keith Robertson, a young man in his early twenties who had been with the Society in England for at least a year and had featured prominently in the charging of several mountains throughout the British Isles following the initial charge on Holdstone Down. Together, these five became the original Founder-Directors of The Aetherius Society in America when, on November 22nd, 1960, the Society was officially incorporated as a nonprofit, religious, scientific and educational organization in the State of California with its new headquarters in Hollywood.

Since that time, Hollywood had become Dr. King's primary residence and the major base of Aetherius Society operations. He and Monique, who he married in 1971, frequently returned to England for a few months during the summer to further his work in that part of the world. Both headquarters continued to steadily grow throughout Dr. King's lifetime although, due to the advanced nature of the teachings and the strong emphasis on service, the Society never became large. For most people it was simply beyond both their capacity to understand and their inclination to find out more.

While Dr. King no doubt would have liked a larger organization in that it would have enabled him to do more, in certain ways he was essentially a private man who disliked a public image and to that extent a small organization that he could easily manage, and where he knew all those around him, was probably far more to his liking.

In terms of finances the Society had always done most things, certainly in the early years, on a shoestring and the lifestyle of almost everyone, including Dr. King and his closest staff, was extremely modest. And yet in a spiritual and karmic way, it had always somehow managed to have enough to achieve its objectives though often extracting significant hardship upon Dr. King, Monique, Irène, Charles, and Al Young, another wonderful soul from the earliest days of The Aetherius Society in America.

All these people were still very active when Pete and I arrived, together with other such legendary characters as Edna Spencer who, in point of fact, had encountered the Master before any of the others at a lecture he gave in Detroit on a cross-country tour of the United States from New York where, in June, 1959, he had arrived with Keith on his way to the UFO conference in Los Angeles the following month. Edna subsequently went on to found the Detroit (later Eastern USA) Branch of the Society and several of the staff in Los Angeles had originated from there having encountered the Society through Edna's outstanding gift for promotion and her infectious enthusiasm for the teachings.

As mentioned earlier, the headquarters could not have been made up of more friendly and accommodating people, and it was all these, no different from those I had encountered in England, who had been drawn together by Dr. King over the previous three decades by the force of his magnetism as a Spiritual Master and the inspiration of the cosmic teachings that he had brought through in his remarkable and indeed unique role of "Primary Terrestrial Mental Channel."

As promised, the "grand tour" was duly arranged within a couple of days and for the first time I had the opportunity to shake his hand and exchange a few pleasant words. It was all very relaxed and yet balanced on a knife's edge of excitement. I had finally met my Master. The tour was fairly straightforward except for one interesting incident. Inside one of the buildings we entered a windowless, air-conditioned room. As we stepped inside to encounter row upon row of reel-to-reel tapes, Dr. King described the contents simply as, "The greatest occult library in the world." Here, literally, was a recording of almost every cosmic transmission he had received over the course of the past 35 years together with innumerable lectures and addresses on metaphysical subjects that he had given since the earliest days in Los Angeles. Rather dumbfounded yet looking for something suitable to say, I said, "Money couldn't buy it, Master," to which he replied, smilingly, "It's not for sale!" And with that, I think it fair to say we'd had our first actual conversation; brief, but a good topic and inside the greatest occult library in the world.

More importantly, at least for myself, the ice was broken. It had been a wonderful encounter, a baptism again only this time by the Master himself. From here, Pete and I could truly immerse ourselves in our American experience.

The American headquarters in Hollywood in the 1970s

Chapter 7

A Fork in the Road

I did not see our Master again until a day or two later. Our visit coincided with the printing of his latest book *Contact With A Lord Of Karma* and the pages were laid out on tables in the temple where a number of us walked in large circles collating them for binding. To everyone's surprise during the evening, Dr. King entered through the side door directly across a small compound from his own home. He looked to my eyes to be somewhat disheveled, never of course having seen him this way and I was about to remark, as if he didn't already know, that his shirt was un-tucked.

Fortunately I restrained myself, perhaps because he had already taken a jovial lunge at me in playful combat, much to the delight of the others. While I didn't react to his move, he then made the very touching gesture of placing his hands over my head almost directly in front of an altar to six Interplanetary Masters, saying: "There you go, boy, there's your crown."

It was a strange incident that brought a change to the atmosphere, and it is only hindsight that has allowed me to see how complimentary that was without knowing its significance, should there even be any. Nonetheless, at the time, it certainly helped me to feel accepted as part of his staff, like an animal's instinct for one of its own.

As the days wore on I remember asking Pete if he would move permanently to Los Angeles if he had the chance. After considering the question as Pete always did, a glass of bourbon and cigarette in his hand, he said, "No" on the grounds that he had a wife and business in London and was very settled with that. It wasn't an issue he needed to consider. Still, he returned the question that, although I hadn't previously asked myself, I replied without pause, bourbon and cigarette in my hand, that I would. It was a propitious moment without knowing how prophetic it was soon to turn out.

With many things always unfolding in Dr. King's life, he had recently received a mental transmission of particular importance regarding the future orbits of a space satellite around Earth. To celebrate this event a special luncheon was arranged, due to take place just a few days after Pete and my departure to London. While we made plans to delay our return other plans were made for John Holder, an International Director in London, to fly over for the occasion as an official representative from the European headquarters.

I had meanwhile moved onto the property to sleep in Irène's small apartment to take care of her two dogs as she had returned to Belgium to visit her mother. Besides having an unusual out-of-body experience similar to one I had experienced when sleeping in The Retreat a few months earlier, this opportunity gave me greater exposure to Lady Monique than I would have otherwise had.

Unaware of the deeper machinations of the headquarters, she lacked a personal assistant and something had caused her to consider that I might be a suitable candidate. Not knowing me well enough to pose such a direct question, she was nonetheless able to ask John more about me once he arrived from London. John, I can only presume, gave a favorable impression and later divulged to myself what Lady Monique had been thinking. I was able to tell him, without even a second thought and in the light of my earlier conversation with Pete, that I would accept the position, surprising John as much with my answer as I had been by his question.

The Divinity shaping my end had just marked out a major incision, myself not oblivious to the wisdom that opportunities taken at the right time for the right reason can indeed lead on to much greater things. By the same token, do the mills of God grind slowly and exceedingly small. Should this indeed come to pass, my compulsion and sincerity for my spiritual path were once again being tested and, rightly or wrongly, not found to be wanting. Moreover, I felt pretty sure of the gamble I was taking, or at least was willing to take.

When word leaked out in England that such an opportunity had been presented, one staff member remarked with something of a rueful smile that I was "a lamb for the slaughter." Yes, I was up for it, even though I did not rightfully know what to expect save to say that others in the past had indeed fallen from such positions of closeness to the Master and that, more to the point, it was well known that Lady Monique was not by any means an easy person to work with. Little did I know, however, what to expect when I returned to Winecellars at the end of the month.

In my absence, Nick—God bless him—had quiet plans of his own being anxious to hand over more of the reins to both myself and another colleague by offering us directorships of the firm and ten percent of its worth. By all accounts, it was not just a tempting offer, it was all any young man needed to advance in the business world of wine. For me, though, and as Nick was soon to find out, it was a slight spanner in the works.

Given this fateful fork in the road as my journey through life became more firmly rooted, it was necessary for me to fully divulge my situation to Nick. Though a little knocked back, he nonetheless was aware of how deeply I had drunk from The Aetherius Society chalice and gracefully acknowledged the potential alternative offer I had been made while in Los Angeles. Naturally enough, he asked when I would know for certain the outcome of this possibly impending move. Not knowing the answer but now under pressure to find out, I asked if he would allow me one month to enquire. While he agreed to this request given that he was in no immediate rush, behind the scenes I learned that his two fellow directors were a little less tolerant of my response.

I immediately informed both Richard Lawrence and John Holder of my predicament, leaning on them to find out more accurate details from Los Angeles and how definite this offer really was. They kindly played their parts and did what they could in this very uncertain situation, about which the Master himself, in all probability, knew nothing. The month went by without any confirmation or even indication from Los Angeles even though, to the best of my understanding, the possibility still stood. Needing to give my answer to Nick, the very best of souls and a man who, with a tiny handful of others, tends to conjure up great affection whenever I think of him, I was at least temporarily still caught between two stools and was thus forced to ask—shame upon my audacity—if Nick would permit me a second month. Since he had few other options, with some reluctance he granted my wish causing even greater consternation behind the closed doors of head office.

The second month passed no differently from the first without a definite confirmation being made from Los Angeles. Therefore, upon Richard and John's best advice, I returned to Nick, cap in hand, and gratefully accepted his original offer, apologizing for all the delay I had caused. His smile and relief showed themselves in the uncorking of a fine bottle of Champagne and the shaking of hands. It was not in my heart what I had most wanted to do but it was, shall we say, a step further upwards in the material world. It would, too, have given my parents great comfort and a similar sigh of relief.

And then, the very next day, word reached Richard in London that Lady Monique still stood by the idea. Los Angeles was still on. At that time, and even upon reflection, I really had no alternative. As hard as it was, I mounted the long climb of stairs to Nick's office, knocked on the door and confessed myself. In a very one-sided conversation, I, with profound apology and genuine regret and even remorse, withdrew my acceptance, and acknowledged fully, that no matter what the final outcome from Los Angeles, the offer previously so generously made no longer remained on the table. So long as there was a shred of a chance to go to America I would take it, no matter what the consequences or the advice and opinions of others. I knew, as if it were something I had known from before I was born, it was a role I had to take, conjuring up another favorite line from *Hamlet*:

> ... *I do not know*
> *Why yet I live to say, "This thing's to do";*
> *Sith I have cause and will and strength and means*
> *To do't...*

And so it was.

I always felt sorry for Nick for letting him down in this way but knowing him to be a man of great depth and heart I am sure he understood, however regrettable to himself. The other colleague who accepted the offer went on to become a Master of Wine and the highly successful founder of one of the largest wine companies in the UK.

In October 2022 I received an invitation from Nick's two daughters to attend his memorial service. He had died aged 82 the previous month, receiving a full-page obituary in The London Times. *I drank a fine bottle of Nebbiolo in his honor and cried as I gave him my own private testimonial. I was later told that he had been more than ready to meet his maker.*

Chapter 8

Moving to America

And so the summer and autumn months of 1989 passed by; nothing definite from Los Angeles but the chance still very real. Then, in January the following year on another routine maintenance trip to The Retreat, word came through that the offer was at long last confirmed. The Master had approved the idea and I should apply for a visa to the United States.

Even then, more than a decade before the terror attacks of "9/11," one could not just walk into the United States of America for a prolonged period of time. The Society in the past had other staff members enter the country under an H-3 training visa and the same was sought for myself. The application papers were duly submitted and I made several visits to the American embassy in Grosvenor Square. They seemed strangely dubious of my reason for travel such that Richard Lawrence kindly donned aspects of his bishop's attire to assist me in convincing the interrogator that I was indeed part of a church, seeking entry to the United States for ministerial training.

Richard's presence and forcefulness won the day and a visa was granted for one year as of April, 1990. My apartment in Treport Street which I would no longer be able to afford was sold to a fellow staff member and, as the final preparations were made to leave, sadness — and even a heaviness — fell upon my family and friends. Paul was finally going, and going into the unknown; and it all appeared as a worrying mistake of life's purposes. And yet they each loved and accepted me to the extent that they knew I was my own man, and to try and persuade me otherwise was as much futile as potentially wrong. Those dearest to me would miss me greatly, and even when a farewell party was held for them in my parents' home there was no discounting the air of sorrow which lay in their hearts. But I, as before, was a man on a mission and the calling had been made. I had to follow.

I arrived in America with three heavy suitcases in hand on Sunday, May 13th, 1990, almost one year later to the day than when I had arrived with Pete. As such, it all looked much the same as if I had never left: the strange purple blossom of the jacaranda trees, the dry heat and the sunshine. Only this time I was alone, no companionship of Pete, and I was here for a year. Who knows, maybe for a lot longer if things went well? I settled in as best I could but they were difficult days and lonely ones. No longer was I a visitor sought out by all; I was a part of the team and, if I was to survive, then I would need to stand on my own two feet and make my own way.

As forewarned, working for Lady Monique as her assistant was not easy. She was tired, drained by a long and constant life at the side of an unrelenting Master who, though in name and practice her husband, was constantly surrounded by others who jostled for his attention. It had been this way for almost thirty years by the time I arrived, allowing me to better understand the earlier warning and the challenges of the position. But still, I was up for it. I liked Lady Monique, somehow feeling sorry for her and I also respected her for her outstanding contribution to the great legacy of The Aetherius Society. Moreover, I was both devoted and determined to taste the crystal waters of the fountainhead for myself as much as possible, independent of what had gone on before; and while I was still well separated from any really meaningful relationship with my Master, I was at the same time only feet away no longer separated by thousands of miles.

With such reassurance and determination I found my way even though, had I doubted myself and looked down, I almost certainly would have fallen to a place where others had fallen before. "Doubt is a killer" had always been one of the Master's sayings. Thankfully, I was never inclined to put it to the test. As such, as the weeks turned to months I slowly became a part of the American headquarters, the inevitable expiry of my H-3 visa always looming above my head.

The Immigration and Naturalization Services required me to return to the UK in April, 1991, but this was not part of our plan. Fortunately, the visa can be renewed for a second year if reliable circumstances have prevented the completion of the training. We made our case based on the sickness of the senior training minister, Charles, which was initially turned down. However, a legitimate and convincing appeal made our case and, to my great relief, the extension was granted.

By this time I had made slight but steady inroads into our Master's routine being not only young and reasonably capable but present at all times of the day. As such he used me for lesser purposes and errands which, so long as I could perform them with reliability, helped assure me my place. He had also taken the time and trouble to learn more about me, inviting me to dinner both with Lady Monique present but also, when she returned in the summer to Belgium, on my own. They were memorable and privileged experiences not commonly offered to his staff.

One especially notable incident was when he called me into his office one morning to ask if I would stay in his home while he was away at Lake Powell in Arizona over the forthcoming weeks. I naturally agreed feeling somewhat honored by the request and I recall that as I turned to leave he added, "You can use the bedroom." I looked back to acknowledge the remark with a quiet, "Thank you." I did not think too much of it other than appreciating that it was a kind and thoughtful gesture.

A few days later, upon his departure, I went across the road to my own apartment to collect my bedding and other items I would need for this temporary stay. I couldn't recall ever having been in the Master's bedroom before and, despite its unfamiliar and rather cold feel, I nonetheless laid down my mattress in view of his added comment which, upon reflection, had seemed an invitation that I would be wise to accept.

Much later that day after we had knocked-off for the night, instead of crossing the road as was normal, I returned to the Master's empty home feeling rather like an intruder in this unfamiliar environment. I remember watching his television for a short time as a way of settling in before retiring to the bedroom. It was all unusual and yet it retained an exotic feeling, knowing that I was entrusted to be in the Master's home and bedroom alone. Lying down, I read for a brief period before turning out the light and then, settling my head upon the pillow, I closed my eyes. Within moments all that I recall was that I had entered the cosmic vastness of outer space! It was an astounding experience that I knew I couldn't take in, virtually short-circuiting my brain. It was all just long enough to have witnessed before I was cast into a deep and profound sleep.

It was not so much bizarre as an understanding of where our Master's mind would go at night; and I felt, or believed, that he had known I would have such an experience hence his earlier parting comment, almost made as a gesture of his appreciation for my doing him a minor but important favor.

I remained in the bedroom for almost three weeks all without further incident. That was until the final morning of the day he was due to return. It was another of those half-awake, half-asleep experiences as I lay in a dreamlike state. As I did so I felt the Master's presence and he was imparting to me "the most important thing." As I became cognizant of the communication I was given images of others walking beside him within a garden and with whom he had a far greater knowledge but who were not always the most cooperative. Despite my being young, even naive, and relatively unknown to him what mattered above all was this most important attribute.

He signaled it to me in a way similar to the experience I had had in my own bedroom in London over five years before by repeating it like a mantra, over and over again. The most important thing was "Attitude... Attitude... Attitude." The impressed implication was that a positive, willing, cheerful attitude was more valuable to our Master, at least at this time in his life, than the length of one's experience or past achievements. Clearly, it was an important lesson for myself and, as much, for all those who would come in the future.

My three-week experience in his home and especially in his bedroom had been marked by these two experiences both coming at the very beginning and end of my brief stay.

Meanwhile, as the months wore on, I had begun to increasingly find my place as an established member of the Los Angeles staff team and headquarters. I had certainly achieved that initial objective of both knowing and being known by the Master. But was it all enough? The year's extension of my H-3 visa was winding down. If I was to remain further another way needed to be found.

With only weeks left before the inevitable expiry of my visa, action had to be taken. It was primarily my problem but by the same token, no one wanted me to go; there was no ousting me out. People, the Master and Lady Monique very much included, wanted me to stay. And so with no other real or legal alternative, upon the Master's suggestion I visited a lawyer specializing in immigration. A member kindly drove me to his office in the valley north of Los Angeles and our conversation began. While this was all new and unfamiliar territory to myself, it was routine to the lawyer, Bernie Sidman. We skated around the topic of the annual lottery before he asked me what I had been doing in Los Angeles. When I told him I worked for a church he almost fell off his chair.

Just days beforehand, if not even hours, and indeed so recently that no paperwork was available, the Immigration and

Naturalization Services had issued an entirely new visa for religious workers. It was all I needed, and with Bernie's help I became one of the very first, if not the actual first in the country, to obtain this R-1 visa which was good for three years and extendable by a further two. At the time it was hard to qualify it all in its rightful context but the Divinity shaping my end had just steered me in the best of all possible directions and it is hard for me to accept that my Master, behind the scenes, had not had a hand in it all. And so I was able to stay in America with a whole new lease of life at least for the next three years, and possibly five. However, the next hurdle arose at the end of the year through a change in ownership of the apartment block across the street where I had been staying.

The new owners naturally needed to know who was living in each of the apartments based upon their own records and, for reasons too complex to explain, we were not the named occupants and, as such, the rent which was paid by the Society in England was set to almost double. This was more than they could rightfully afford and, so again, my status in America came into question. The Master offered me the use of his motorhome which I was ready to accept but others were less convinced of this move.

As the wheels turned it was decided to relieve a fellow full-time employee, Alan Moseley, of his accommodation on the church property when the Master was in residence and offer the room to myself since Alan also had a home of his own in the neighborhood. It was all round a beneficial move although one direct consequence was that I was to become, in place of Alan, both a healer of our Master and someone required to help put him to bed alongside Brian and Richard Medway. It also meant that I would become, together with Brian, the other resident on the property and aide to our Master, someone to be called upon at any time of the night. Not only was it a new experience for both myself and the Master, it would definitely be a stepping up to the plate which, despite all my intent and desire, I hardly felt prepared for this role.

An early test came along all too soon. The Master had been in bed for about twenty minutes when he called over the intercom for assistance. Brian and I both arrived to discover that he wanted to change his pajamas. After a quick search in the bedroom for another pair, Brian realized that the ones we were seeking were in the motorhome and he went off to fetch them. This left me alone with the Master lying in his bed. It was an awkward moment, at least for myself, as neither of us spoke.

As the minutes ticked by and I wondered what could possibly be taking Brian so long, I decided to stand outside in the passageway relieving the pressure of the silence. To my great consternation it must have taken Brian at least ten minutes to return from the parking lot outside and as he walked into the bedroom clutching the pajamas, myself innocently following on behind, instead of asking Brian what had taken him so long, the Master looked directly at me and demanded, rather angrily, "Where on earth have you been!?"

I have not forgotten the incident that, strangely, was not without irony. Over the remaining years of the Master's life, I was to spend hundreds of hours with him alone in his bedroom.

Chapter 9

At the Master's Side

Over the following year, 1993, I continued to serve as an aide to our Master supporting Brian and Richard whenever the Master was in Los Angeles which was roughly fifty percent of the year, alternating his two to three weekly visits with his home in Santa Barbara. Then, on January 17th, 1994, at 4:30 a.m. the Northridge earthquake struck Los Angeles County and my life with the Master for the rest of his days forever changed.

The 6.7 quake had jolted his house off its foundations and the subsequent retrofitting of the building, together with major upheavals all around the headquarters, forced him to take refuge in Santa Barbara. On the weekend of February 19th and 20th I was requested to relieve Richard and Brian for a day off, expecting to return to Los Angeles early the following week.

However, in simple terms I never returned and apart from the very occasional visit, nor did the Master. From that significant event of the earthquake, the Master's home in Santa Barbara became the Temporary Command headquarters of The Aetherius Society and remained so for the rest of Sir George's life—a life which ended almost three and a half years later at 4:48 a.m. on Saturday, July 12th, 1997.

From those earliest days, more than ten years beforehand, when I first learned of Dr. King and his unique cosmic teachings, through my joining the staff team in London and my early concern of ever meeting my Master, I had become one of his full-time aides, even earning the nickname "Mostly" since, in his own words during the latter months of his life, he would often say, "It's mostly Paul I want."

Moreover, I was among just a handful of people who not only lived with the Master but knew him very closely. It was by all accounts, a remarkable privilege but in another way, as I reflect upon these things more than ten years later, one of the great things I knew before I was born.

Inevitably, it allowed me to have remarkably personal experiences and insights of our Master who I increasingly came to love, not so much as a Master—which he undoubtedly was—but, simply as George King; an old-fashioned, traditional Englishman with a down-to-earth and inherently good-natured outlook upon life. It adhered me to him deeply and, I would like to think, it was somewhat mutual.

As such, I was used more and more for the most un-cosmic like of duties; mundane even, but all with a gentle sweetness as he ran down the final episode of his life. However, there were still unusual events that kept one ever mindful of his true status. One in particular stands out. I was on duty overnight which meant that his beeper was moved into my room should he need any assistance which inevitably he would, possibly on and off throughout the night bringing little sleep.

Sometime after midnight not long after we had put him to bed, I heard the sound of his mechanical bed being raised. This was nothing unusual, in fact totally to be expected; just a slight dismay that it should occur so soon after he had supposedly fallen asleep. I awaited the inevitable sound of the buzzer. Almost a minute passed without it being depressed. This was strange so I cracked open my bedroom door, mystified as to why it had not gone off. Then, even more mysteriously, I saw him enter his bathroom. This was not just strange, it was unheard of. Never did he arise from his bed without our assistance. What on earth could be going on?

I closed the door and lay on my bed somewhat perplexed. A few minutes later I heard him coming out of the bathroom and then I could literally "feel" him coming down the passageway alongside where I was lying on the bed. Surely he was going to open my bedroom door, but no. Instead, I felt myself becoming paralyzed unable to move a muscle. This strange and most unexpected feeling gradually dissipated as he carried on down the passageway. Then, I sensed him turning around coming back down towards the bathroom. Again, my body became increasingly rigid until he passed by. It was all utterly bizarre, and then I felt him coming back down for a second time. Again, I became completely paralyzed unable to move a limb before he turned around to head back down towards the bathroom rendering me totally immobile a second time as he passed by. Then, for a third time, he came back down all with the same experience as before.

I can only surmise that he had been in important communication with one of the Masters and the last thing he needed was an interruption from myself. The only other possible explanation I can give is that he had let down part of his aura for whatever reason. It was all as strange as it was remarkable and yet, with respect for his privacy, I never mentioned it and nor did he. It was just one of those exceptional experiences of what it was to live under the same roof as the Master.

As I wrote at the outset, it is part of my life to speak of these things — not so much my involvement which in the grand scheme of things was minimal and not worthy of mention; but why the life and work of His Eminence Sir George King has been, and indeed remains, the most profoundly significant factor in the fundamental changing of our world and in the lives of us all as we prepare for a New Awakening and the Dawning of a New World upon Terra.

Part II:

A Cosmic Scripture for the New World

If you tell the truth in a way that it can be understood, it will be believed.
William Blake, Poet

Lies go with the wind. Truth can go against the wind.
Swami Vivekananda, Hindu Saint

He that hath ears to hear, let him hear.
Jesus Christ

*Dedicated to
my Spiritual Master,
His Eminence Sir George King,
and the Cosmic Master,
Aetherius.*

Dr. George King

Chapter 1

Maldek and Extraterrestrial Life

Part I of this book (*The Things I Knew Before I Was Born*) began with a reference to Maldek. It is difficult to make more than a reference to this defining moment in our past in the same way that it is difficult for us to remember and define our own birth. Yes, we were there; and yes, it was a pivotal moment in our existence, but we were not sufficiently cognizant to take in the details, or even any of the details. Without being told how we were born and how we emerged into the world, we would not know.

And so it is, up to a point, with Maldek. In a way it was our collective beginning despite it being an actual end, and an explanation as to how and why we came to be here upon Earth. Similarly, this collective beginning should be a pivotal and defining question that is asked by each and every one of us as a species. Earth is our common home in the vastness of all space about which we are increasingly learning how small we are and, when seen in that way, how insignificant we are in the universe. Indeed, the best we can do in terms of understanding our origins as to how and whence we came to be here at all is to rely upon myth.

Among the best known of these myths, certainly in the Western world, is that of the Garden of Eden from which stem the three great Abrahamic faiths, steeped themselves in their own stories. One can even make the case that preceding Abraham and his wife, Sarah, was Brahma and his wife, Saraswati, who originated from the even more ancient legends of India and Hinduism. Either way, as with all myths that have endured throughout the ages, they can have their roots in a certain truth.

The "paradise" of Eden from which we fell relates, at least in part, to Maldek; a planet we destroyed over 18,000,000 years ago. All that remains of Maldek is the asteroid belt, countless pieces of lifeless rock orbiting between Mars and Jupiter.

I do not wish to make an astronomical argument for Maldek save to say that the discovery of a gigantic iron core as the possible basis of a planet, combined with the location of these asteroids falling exactly into the remarkable numerical sequence of Bode's Law as to where a planet might expect to be found, both give credence to these giant pieces of floating rock having once formed a planet.

The metaphysical understanding as detailed in the Akashic records, an ethereal account of everything, is that Maldek was destroyed through the intense misuse of atomic power, far more cataclysmic than our present-day potential although we may only be decades away, or less, from attaining a similar capability.

The other important premise besides Maldek to which this book subscribes is the existence of extraterrestrial life, not just in the physical sense of UFOs but to be seen within a metaphysical and spiritual context. Indeed, one can only comprehend this story by embracing an understanding that not only does "God" exist as a unifying Divine Principle, but that life is manifesting on multitudinous dimensions. It is a fundamental principle; indeed, the original principle from which all else in creation stems.

It is this singular Divine Intelligence which is behind the "Big Bang," that primordial sound which the ancients of the East knew as the sacred A-U-M. It is referred to in the Bible as "the Word" that, in the beginning, was God; a beginning from which all else arose at least 13,000,000,000 years ago.

This all-embracing, all-encompassing original birth is more gracefully described by the yogis as the great "out-breathing of God" for which, they conceive, there must be a reciprocal "in-breathing" in which all creation will be returned. This must provoke the inevitable and fascinating question, "For how long has this God been breathing?"

We are all part of some unknowable Whole that arose out of an apparent Nothingness and Nowhere only to be returned "in full consciousness," as per the yogis who appear to grasp these things, to that same original Whole from which it all began. It is difficult to consider or conceive of any other greater idea for not only is there a logic in such an understanding but, equally, it contains an innate beauty epitomized by the youthful poet, John Keats, when he wrote: "Beauty is Truth, truth beauty," before adding: "that is all ye know on earth, and all ye need to know."

Against this vast cosmic backdrop the fall of Maldek is relatively recent and, one might even argue, equally insignificant; only that nothing in creation is or ever can be completely insignificant for in the wholeness of everything even the fall of a sparrow is known, just as each of the hairs on our heads is numbered in the Mind of God.

Chapter 2

Freewill and All That

Further to understanding this story, this ultimate and only story—this myth narrative about which we can only really speculate through the process of deep meditative thought and with a full and unrestrained heart, it becomes apparent (harking back to the Garden of Eden) that within this all-inclusive, ever-expanding universe of God exists what we call "freewill."

It is the allowance for alternate and even deviant thought; the option to choose and the audacity to act upon that choice which, in and of themselves, opens us up to the mirage of a false god in which we may perceive ourselves to be separate from the actual God. And when and once that move is made and given credence, the reaction is to find ourselves naked and exposed as in the original sin born from an illusion out of ignorance.

The experience of this perceived, separate identity invokes a previously unforeknown sensation of guilt that equally, in our apparent nakedness, we attempt to disguise with an experiment of lies and from here the great unravelling begins.

In horribly simple terms, it is this scenario albeit with imagery we can hopefully understand that lies at the basis of our state of being in the world today, and dating all the way back to a time before the destruction of Maldek.

At some point in our distant past we chose freewill, reinforcing this perception of our separation from God; and, as we continued to unfurl, we solidified our new identity with an arrogance and denial. We complicated ourselves in bizarre and perverse ways. Science became dominant as we began to seek dominance over each other, developing technologies that appeared to enhance ourselves over our neighbor. In the end we devised atom bombs which we unleashed, annihilating ourselves and, in the case of Maldek, our world.

This was our past fraught with illusion, lies and deception all grounded in ignorance. In one sense it can appear as an entrancing game but, like an addict, we had created for ourselves a scenario from which it was difficult to find release; and yet all the while we were bound by the inescapable Law of God, called "Karma," which encases everything.

Karma is not just an all-pervasive law of balance and counterbalance but, even more demanding, it is the inevitable Law of God. While we may choose freewill, we can never truly separate ourselves from God; for God is the Beginning and the End and everything in between. Indeed, in the context of eternity, this ever-breathing God is even the stage *before* the Beginning and the stage *after* the End. The prison of freewill is a prism within the Mind of God as an aspect of this all-embracing, all-encompassing singular Being only we haven't yet realized or remembered it.

Following the destruction of Maldek we could not simply end it all. Throw in the cards so to speak as a failed experiment, as if it was all a game of poker and we had just lost; for God not only owns the house, God is the house and sets the rules. For that reason, one might be quick to assume that this all-encompassing God is a tyrant overlord from whom no escape is possible, but such a consideration would not only be horribly wrong, it would also be to take hold of the wrong end of the stick, a position we have been taking for a long, long time.

For God and karma, in their mercy, are not cruel but the absolute, supreme expression of Love; and this inevitable journey we are all making from before the Beginning to after the End is for us to become fully conscious of our divine nature as an inseparable aspect of this thing called God, from which we cannot ever escape.

There is no real alternate explanation, unless one chooses to believe in nihilism which is merely to prolong the process if not the agony. For those who do profess such a philosophy, I suspect the words on these pages are not for them; but if you are curious to know more about this cosmic voyage we are all taking, then you are encouraged to continue. For we are living in an accelerated time when an increased demand to know such truth is calling out, and even though this has always been the way, the urgency for us to change—as individuals and collectively— has now, almost suddenly, become incumbent upon us all.

Despite the destruction of Maldek over 18,000,000 years ago, it was not possible for us simply to be taken out of creation. We are an aspect of creation and the Divine Spark exists within us all. As such, another planet within this solar system, presumably for karmic reasons, needed to be found from whence we could continue this evolutionary journey back to the source from which we had come at the beginning of time. The options were few for all the other planets were already too advanced for us "Maldekians," the destroyers of a world. Freewill had never been a path that they had taken.

In saying that, it is necessary to clarify again that in this understanding of our story, more and even less evolved life exists throughout all creation on varying degrees of vibrational dimension both above and below this physical realm upon which we ourselves exist.

And so, at some point after the fall of Maldek, the highly evolved life-force—or "Logos"—of Earth was approached and she agreed, with divine self-sacrifice, to allow our continued rebirth upon her body albeit under tremendous karmic limitation and in a far deeper state of involution. There are consequences to all action that cannot simply be brushed aside or forgiven. It is an important aspect to understand and goes somewhat contrary to the Christian belief that Christ forgave us our sins. Transgression, or sin born out of ignorance, cannot simply be forgiven without some form of recompense for, using Jesus' own words, "As you sow, so must you reap."

This is an explanation of karma, like that given by the Buddha who similarly stated, "Action and Reaction are opposite and equal." Our sins cannot simply be ignored, brushed aside, or forgiven. All action needs to be balanced and when we act in the correct way, according to our conscience as directed by Divine Will rather than our freewill, we reap the consequence in such a way that we are moved forward in our journey. This is a fundamental concept and essential to understand if we are to realize not only our true purpose as human beings but in helping to save our world.

Chapter 3

Lemuria, Atlantis and our Modern World

And so, at some point over 18,000,000 years ago we resumed our evolutionary journey upon Earth through the slow process of reincarnation, all in this divine process of reuniting with God in the fullness of time, and with a complete realization of all that this means.

What all that this means, again according to the ancient yogis, is for This to know That; or in other words, for the manifested universe to know Itself as God. It can seem hard to understand or qualify as to why That would seemingly create a manifestation of Itself merely to know Itself. One simple way I try to explain it is in recalling the time many years ago when I had seen a movie and my housemate had not. I remember saying to him, "I envy you for not having seen this movie." My reason being was that he did not know what delight awaited him.

I believe it is the same for us. This journey we are all taking is about the experience of ever-expanding consciousness and bliss; an elevation of every aspect of our whole being to ever-increasing heights infinitely beyond our wildest imaginings.

The traditional thinking is that the attainment of earthly Enlightenment as demonstrated by the Buddha was our ultimate state of being, referred to in Sanskrit as Nirvana. But the cosmic teachings of George King that have, in part, been given by himself as a trained yogi and, more significantly, communicated through him by intelligences from higher dimensions beyond this world indicate that Nirvana is not so much the ultimate state but rather the true beginning of our real existence. It is a stage we have not yet reached, save for a tiny handful of individuals.

Attaining to this state is our primary purpose for being on Earth and yet we hamper ourselves through the continual misuse of freewill. Thus it demands our need for living life after life after life through the seemingly endless process of reincarnation, all of which is governed by the inescapable Law of Karma. Realization of this ultimate purpose is especially needed at this time, not just for our own sake but if we are to reorientate how we are living upon this planet in order to survive.

To better understand these times and the accelerating changes taking place, we need to again look back into our past. Having found ourselves slowly evolving out of the involution we had karmically demanded following the destruction of Maldek, we emerged into the civilization of Lemuria as recorded in the Akashic record. It was a long, slow process towards becoming intelligent beings, but the "disease" of freewill remained and with it came the same lust for power and dominance that had caused our downfall upon Maldek. And in the end the weapons of war were unleashed again, destroying Lemuria and all semblance of life as we knew it.

Again, the slow process of reincarnation stepped in under the all-guiding hands of karma in their mercy and grace as we continued this inevitable process of reaching for the light.

How long ago this all was is difficult to say and does not necessarily matter, but one would estimate at least one or two million years. We had destroyed ourselves and our world was made uninhabitable, but we had not destroyed the planet. Over the following hundreds of thousands of years, possibly more, the evolutionary process continued until, once more, we developed into an advanced technological race within a civilization known as Atlantis.

As with Lemuria, there are various myths about this time in our distant past, among the best known being attributed to Plato.

And then, as you will have known or otherwise surmised, Atlantis fell no differently to Lemuria before. Both had been destroyed by an unleashing of hatred and atomic power although without the same full force that had occurred upon Maldek. Humanity, for all its scientific capabilities, had been unable to rid itself of our more basic nature. One could even be forgiven for thinking that we were doomed to failure but, as we again know from the poets, the mills of God grind slowly but they grind exceeding small. Whatever our plans, God, in its origins, has other plans and no matter our own thinking we cannot ultimately escape those grinding mills.

All of which, somewhat loosely, brings us to the present day. As I have said, the details of Maldek, Lemuria and Atlantis are too long ago to know for sure, and hard evidence is scant; and so, beyond an ability to read the Akashic records, we must take them largely on faith. But it need not be a blind faith for as the American existentialist, Ralph Waldo Emerson, wonderfully wrote, "All I have seen teaches me to trust the Creator for all that I have not seen." It is an inspired consideration.

The teachings and thoughts put forward for this modern age by the yogi adept George King and the extraterrestrial intelligences who spoke through him provide sound evidence that allow us to take these obscure concepts more fully on board.

Other compelling testimony has to be the clear evidence of flying saucers, now known as UAPs (unidentified aerial phenomena), together with manifestations such as crop circles that have been appearing with increasing regularity in remarkable formations and in unknown ways, both of which should force us to take all these things with an earnest seriousness.

In short, our world is being changed not just by the swirling activity of rampant humanity but by forces beyond our skies. It is time for all of us to step up and take notice.

Chapter 4

Flying Saucers and Their Message

This book is not a treatise on the craft we know as "flying saucers," a term coined in 1947 by Kenneth Arnold, an American aviator who witnessed several flying discs over Washington State that resembled upturned saucers. In fact, these craft had been sighted throughout the recently ended World War II and were referred to by pilots as "foo fighters." It is understood that one particularly spectacular sighting reported by a Royal Air Force crew became immediately classified by Prime Minister Winston Churchill because, he felt, "It would cause mass panic among the population and a disbelief in the church."

When taken from the perspective of the beings inhabiting the higher realms of other planets within our solar system, they had witnessed this long, slow and involved journey of humanity from before the time of Maldek, through Lemuria and Atlantis right up to our present day. Each time they had seen how we had destroyed ourselves through our inability to control our basic nature; this false notion devolved from freewill which gives rise to feelings of fear and lack and, above all, an inherent insecurity born out of a self-imposed ignorance.

During World War II we again unleashed the atom killing over two hundred thousand souls with two bombs to end a war that had already killed more than forty million. In the aftermath came the Cold War in which we went further by developing the infinitely more deadly hydrogen bomb. It was an all-too-familiar scenario to these other beings for whom Oneness was and always had been their own experience. And yet we are a part of that Oneness and with that very same divine essence buried within us. Even more importantly, it all had to be seen within the context of the Earth and the solar system itself.

In the concept of Oneness all manifestation is living, interconnected and evolving. There literally is no separation. Earth and all the planets, even the suns and galaxies are a part of it. It is all alive and conscious, indeed with a consciousness that is billions of years more evolved than our own. And yet we are still a part of it. The destruction of Maldek was not just a matter of saying, "Oh well..." It was an intrinsic part of everything, just as the fall of a sparrow is known and has meaning to God. There was an effect, a consequence, and when we are dealing with something as evolved and life-sustaining as a planet the karmic ramifications stretch far and wide. And all this had been caused by ourselves in the delusion, or "Maya," of freewill; and with that choice we had fallen from Paradise into the "Mire" of our present and previous existences. This is where we find ourselves at this time. This is our story. This is who we are.

It was into this scenario in May, 1954, during the Cold War that a young man named George King emerged as a "voice" for these beings from beyond our world.

Born in Shropshire, England, in 1919, he was of prime fighting age when World War II broke out in Europe twenty years later. However, his conscience knew "Thou shalt not kill" was a timeless law, and instead he chose to serve as a section leader in London's Fire Brigade during the Blitz where he witnessed the bombing of civilians and the collapse of buildings into which he would race to rescue terrified children, babies, and the elderly. The experience had been a defining moment in his own life, prompting him to ask the essential question: "Why?"

In the aftermath he was living and working in London with various jobs including as a driver for a private employer. It was work that allowed him to devote up to eight hours of his day to yogic practice. He was seeking answers to this worldly predicament of atomic insanity and yoga was the path which he took.

His determination was as rare as it was exceptional and nothing less than the goal of yoga, Enlightenment, was his destination. A decade later, he had reached it and with it came mastery. He had prepared himself to help humanity though it was unexpected, even for himself, when he was contacted by an alien intelligence using the name "Aetherius." Neither he nor the world would ever be the same again. He was just 35 years of age.

It is constantly necessary to view this story within a much broader context and by using a cosmic lens; a lens that embraces the whole solar system, our galaxy, and perhaps most of all, Laniakea. Laniakea is a beautiful Hawaiian word literally meaning "immense heaven," and it describes a supercluster of galaxies towards which all life within the vastness of the Milky Way together with over 100,000 other similar galaxies in our sector of the universe is being drawn, all at phenomenal and accelerating speed.

This is what is really going on from the cosmic perspective and has been since the beginning of time, all as a consequence of the great out-breathing of God.

In the Grand Scheme, we are all moving at immeasurable and accelerating speed towards Laniakea which, itself, is moving towards an even more magnificent celestial body. This is the greater reality and we are all a part of it. It is a divine cosmic movement that is infinitely breathtaking, well beyond our capacity to comprehend; and yet it is the future that awaits us. It is the "This" that is in the dance towards knowing the "That" in this great and sublime mystery of life.

It is into this same picture that we can also appreciate that there comes an end to freewill. Not only is that time always pressing but it, too, is being accelerated. It is why this time is so important together with the incumbent need for all of us to become aware of this greater universal reality, and in so doing allow ourselves to be changed in the light of it.

In 1955, one year after that initial contact, George King founded The Aetherius Society as a means of recording and acting upon the information he was starting to receive from other worlds. He had previously been working with a small group in London who used telepathy to gain rapport with a handful of souls existing on the higher realms of this Earth. These are the realms to which we go when we die, awaiting reincarnation. They are not all higher, however. There are also lower realms as depicted in Dante's inferno where we can also go depending on the karmic pattern we have formed in our previous lives.

George King and his group were primarily engaged in healing work, particularly through the use of color vibration. The intelligences who had communicated through him included Doctor Lister, and the scientists Sir James Young Simpson and Sir Oliver Lodge as well as one or two more advanced intelligences who were closely associated with an ancient order of Masters, male and female, who had attained the mystic state of "Samadhi," the highest state of consciousness known to man.

With experience of Samadhi and the ability to attain it at will, these Masters are no longer bound by the karmic wheel of reincarnation having "ascended," a state of evolution we are all destined to ultimately reach. They are known by various terms, the most common being simply "Ascended Masters," and they play a vital role in holding a karmic balance upon Earth. The most elevated of these masters is the Lord Babaji who has literally been here since we came to Earth over 18,000,000 years ago.

This seems to us as a long time, it is a long time; but in cosmic time it is all relative. If we consider Earth to be about four and a half billion years old, were that taken as a 24-hour day then 18,000,000 years represents the last six minutes. Lemuria occurred less than one minute ago and Atlantis within the last few seconds.

Together, these Ascended Masters are also known as the Spiritual Hierarchy of Earth, or the Great White Brotherhood, white having nothing to do with race but with magic, as in the energy which they wield.

Chapter 5

The Masters Speak

When we stand back and view this period of the Cold War into which we had entered immediately after the end of World War II, humanity had once again allowed itself to become deeply divided with fierce political rivalries and mutual fears. In 1962 alone, the staggering equivalent of 12,000 bombs the size of those dropped upon Hiroshima was "tested" throwing tremendous amounts of atomic radiation into the atmosphere.

It was also a time, unsurprisingly, when flying saucer sightings were at an all-time high giving rise to numerous groups of curiously-minded folk springing up across the globe.

Into this same mix came this young man of extraordinary ability. Through tremendous self-discipline and effort borne out of a profound urge to help this forlorn race of humans, George King had recently attained the elevated yogic state of Samadhi with the ability to access the highest aspects of the human mind. It was this capability which allowed him to be contacted by the more evolved intelligences originating from the higher dimensions of this solar system, and who were no less anxious to help humanity, albeit strictly within the bounds of karmic law.

It was these same intelligences who had watched over our destruction of Atlantis. Who, even earlier, had seen how we had perished with the fall of Lemuria; and, going back millions of years, how we had destroyed the planet upon which we had once lived. They could see this dangerous trend repeating itself yet again, all caused by our own folly and ingrained ignorance of this divine journey we are making as the fundamental purpose of our lives.

As the "Cosmic Masters" began to communicate through George King, an inevitable part of their message warned us of the atomic dangers we were creating and how this imperiled not only ourselves but also the planet and the surrounding cosmos. Indeed, so dangerous was this atomic radiation that after the fall of Lemuria these same Masters had erected the ionosphere, or "ring-pass-not," around the Earth as a protective barrier. While this prevented the outward spread of atomic radiation into the cosmos, it also prevented the Earth from receiving vital energies that are essential to her own well-being as a planet. After Atlantis, this protective barrier was intensified, further limiting the flow of these life-sustaining energies from the other planetary bodies within the system.

It may be hard to grasp or accept this philosophy when it has never been part of ordinary terrestrial thought, and yet we need to constantly view this whole predicament through the cosmic lens of Spiritual Oneness. All of creation is alive, emanating from the same Divine Source that arose billions of years ago out of mysterious Infinity. As with ourselves, the Earth is a living intelligence and a part of this same singular manifestation of God. In allowing us to reseed ourselves upon her body following the destruction of Maldek, she brought tremendous limitation upon herself and a slowing down of her own evolutionary journey. Such sacrificial action on a truly cosmic scale was considerably worsened with the erection of the ring-pass-not, essential for our protection but detrimental to herself.

Thus, in the early messages being spoken by the Cosmic Masters through George King they also pointed out that while it was one thing for humanity to destroy itself, we would not be allowed to destroy the planet as we had done with Maldek.

This may have been seen as a long shot at the time yet those same Masters would have known that it might only be a matter of decades before we had discovered the same capability as we had created upon Maldek. Even now, just 60 years later, this journey into the atom is being pursued with intense vigor in underground laboratories in Europe and China where thousands of physicists and other scientists are attempting to harness the full potential of what they call the "God particle."

On January 29th, 1955, a few days after his 36th birthday, George King delivered the first public message originating from the Cosmic Masters in London's Caxton Hall. It was to be one of more than 600 he would receive over the following 25 years. Naturally, interest and curiosity arose in these messages, including by the British government who wondered if he was a communist spy. It was, after all, the height of the Cold War and fear was rampant.

Chapter 6

George King

The Aetherius Society in London soon attracted a small group of intrigued and enthusiastic men and women, young and old, who offered varying degrees of help and support. They had been drawn by the extraordinary messages that were being spoken through George King from intelligences claiming to be from other worlds. It was difficult not to be mystified, especially when some of the transmissions related to flying saucer forecasts that were subsequently verified by people in places all around the globe who could have known nothing of their earlier predictions.

Moreover, the messages had a profundity of wisdom, both practical and spiritual. The fact that they purported to be from alien sources only intensified the curiosity. If they were real, they demanded a radical rethink of just about everything; if they were false, then George King was nothing more than a charlatan. It was a question everyone who heard the messages needed to decide for themselves, but his notoriety spread and before long the attenders at the Caxton Hall numbered in the hundreds, often with standing room only.

Just as this book is not a treatise on flying saucers, it is not a biography of George King. For that, readers are recommended to study his official biography, *The King Who Came To Earth* by Richard Lawrence and Brian Keneipp, published by The Aetherius Society in 2019, the hundredth anniversary of George King's birth.

Over the course of his life George King became known to his followers by various titles from simply George in the early years; Dr. George King when he was awarded a doctorate by a theological seminary in the 1960s; Sir George King when he was knighted by a chivalric order in the late 1970s; and Prince George when he was crowned by a royal house in 1981; as well as His Eminence Sir George King, the official title of an archbishop, which he was created in the previous year. At some point in the late 1980s, most of these titles were set aside and he mainly became known by everyone in The Aetherius Society as "the Master." It is true that none of the other titles came from established organizations that the orthodox world tends to recognize, but by the same token neither were they entirely bogus.

When one begins to see George King as a yoga master, even as an "avatar" as someone who came to this backward world from elsewhere, one can better understand the karmic need for humanity to award him with temporal titles as a reflection of our appreciation. After all, the best we gave Jesus was a "crown of thorns" before we nailed him to a cross and crucified him. The Buddha was made to beg. Even the late Mahatma Gandhi, a noble human being if ever there was one, was described as a "fakir" and a "malignant subversive fanatic" by "Sir" Winston Churchill who represented Gandhi's sovereign rulers. The so-called Establishment has never liked those who appear different and threatening to the social order, and so it was for George King.

None of this especially matters and certainly does not alter the message being given by the Cosmic Masters through him. The fact that he was not recognized by established institutions says more about their disinterest and lack of any serious investigation into George King and his message than it does about him.

Again, when viewed through the much broader cosmic lens, George King can be seen as an avatar who came to Earth at a critical point in our evolution and, far more importantly, the evolution of the planet. He was "one of them" rather than "one of us," although to all intents and purposes he appeared as one of us and chose to live as one of us, albeit in disguise and without ever openly revealing his true identity. It was no doubt easier for him, and besides, he had not come for earthly glamor or fortune. He shied away from publicity, at least for the sake of it, and lived overall very modestly, and often in the early years with financial hardship having, in true yogic tradition, given away all material possession at the outset of his mission.

Besides, purporting to bring through messages from alien beings was never a way to become popular or rich unless, of course, one was indeed a charlatan (and there have been a few), and in which case the riches and the fame do not last for long. This was not George King, not by a long shot.

By 1958 the Society had established a modest headquarters on the Fulham Road in southwest London with a growing and dedicated group of followers. They assisted George King in whatever ways they could, most importantly in recording and transcribing the transmissions as they came through and publishing them in the Society's journal, *Cosmic Voice*, which would be mailed to members and subscribers spread around the world.

Later, in the summer of that same year and in the space of just a few days, two major cosmic events occurred as the Cosmic Masters stepped up their intervention.

The first was the instruction for George King to make his way to a hilltop in southwest England at midnight on July 23rd where he was to have an encounter with Jesus, the very same Master who had lived on Earth two thousand years before. To the orthodox mind this must sound utterly far-fetched and the opportunity to completely dismiss everything about George King and The Aetherius Society, but that is a knee-jerk reaction based on the conditioning of our culture.

To the open mind, it is conceivable that life can and even does exist upon other dimensions within creation including our own solar system. The Aetherius Society believes that this is the case with Jesus having originated from Venus, "the bright and morning star" as he himself states in the Bible. Looked at slightly differently, it makes at least as much sense as Jesus either being eternally dead, especially in the light of the Resurrection, or else living somewhere at the right hand of God. The same can be said for the "Star of Bethlehem" being an extraterrestrial craft rather than a sun hovering over a stable.

The purpose of this meeting was for Jesus to transmit a high frequency of energy through George King acting as a karmic conduit into the ether of space within the hilltop, known locally as Holdstone Down. It is a science beyond our present capabilities but that should not deny its possibility. However, the real test of the pudding is in the eating. The energy transmitted into Holdstone Down was given as a source of enhanced energy for humanity to invoke and send out to the world for peace and inspiration at this critical time of planetary change.

It was the first of nineteen such locations around the world to be charged by the Cosmic Masters in this way, culminating with Le Nid d'Aigle in the French Alps just over three years later. The mission was known as "Operation Starlight," no doubt after that initial meeting upon Holdstone Down at midnight. Jesus was not the only Cosmic Master to transmit the charge of energy through George King into the mountains. There were others including Aetherius, also a Venusian Master, and another intelligence who went by the name of Mars Sector 6, all three of whom had communicated through George King.

Again, it is necessary to understand that we are not talking about the physical plane of these other planets. It is an important metaphysical lesson to recognize that life exists upon other dimensions, including around this Earth where there are both higher and lower realms which we inhabit in an auric body between incarnations. The timeless soul journey we are all making is back to the source, all bound within the universal Law of Karma. We are presently at a very elementary stage with the experience of Nirvana, or Enlightenment, being our destination. Reincarnation and the correct use of freewill allow us to navigate this journey toward this higher state of consciousness.

The second important interaction came just four days later on Sunday, July 27th. Again it was an encounter with the Master Jesus, this time in the basement of the Society's headquarters in London which was used then as it is now as a sanctuary. George King had to follow strict instructions for the prior 24 hours in order to prepare himself for Jesus to deliver what was to become an outstanding series of spiritual teachings. The message was given as a Blessing to those "who work for Peace." It was reminiscent of the Sermon on the Mount he had given two thousand years before and the Blessing was followed with a prayer for the upliftment of humanity.

The following Sunday another Blessing was delivered, this time to "The Wise Ones," those who had found Peace and turned away from it in order to give it to those who had not found it; namely ourselves. Over the following ten weeks a remarkable New Age Bible had been delivered, literally with a Cosmic Concept, giving humanity a far greater understanding of God, referred to as the "Absolute," and the godliness of such beings as the Mother Earth, the Mighty Sun and the Galaxy. It is a profound series of teachings suitably called "The Twelve

Blessings," and it has gone on to change the lives of thousands of people around the world.

With the advent of Operation Starlight and the publication of *The Twelve Blessings*, the terrestrial mission of George King was taking firmer root and with it came a steady expansion of the organization he had founded just three years before based upon the directives of Higher Forces.

Chapter 7

Carnedd Llywelyn and the BBC

Just as George King had been instructed to attend a rendezvous on Holdstone Down in July, 1958, early the following year he was similarly directed by the Cosmic Masters to present himself in the United States for the purpose of extending Operation Starlight and to give their cosmic message to the people of that country.

He made the journey in June, 1959, accompanied by Keith Robertson, a young man in his early twenties who had already joined George King in the charging of several other holy mountains in Britain. Keith was very capable despite his young age, assisting George King in a variety of ways as they traveled together. He was also an excellent public speaker often introducing George King at various lecture halls.

By the time they left Southampton aboard a merchant ship bound for New York, eight more mountains in Operation Starlight had been charged and *The Twelve Blessings* had been published. This was in addition to two other very recent yet significant events.

The first of these was on April 11th, 1959, beneath Carnedd Llywelyn in North Wales, one of the holy mountains that had been charged in Operation Starlight. George King, as a yogi adept, had projected from his physical body to a lower dimension for an encounter with a black magician and the principal architect in the manipulation of forces that had led to the crucifixion of Jesus two thousand years before. During the battle George King was killed in addition to his own transmutation of the evil magician whom he fought.

The Master Aetherius delivered a commentary of the entire action through George King seated in his physical body in

London while, behind the scenes, giving him the choice of either remaining on Earth to continue his mission or to die. George King chose to live on and the cord between life and death was rejoined by the Master Aetherius. It proved to be a very decisive decision, and one which would prove vital for the human race.

Though it was not known outside the handful of Aetherius Society members who had attended the transmission, George King was also a Cosmic Adept, one of three who had taken on a physical body for an essential purpose upon Earth. This was his first taste of battle on the lower astral realms and it had been, literally, a fight to the death with George King ultimately prevailing.

During the time I was privileged to assist in the care of George King at his private home in Santa Barbara in the latter years of his life, I remember discussing with him some of the events that had preceded the Battle on Carnedd Llywelyn. He enjoyed the conversation, the facts of which he already well knew, and he suggested that I give an address on the subject sometime in the future.

This I did on the fortieth anniversary of the battle in 1999, pointing out the unusual sequence of events none of which had been by chance; "coincidence" being a word not included in George King's lexicon.

Carnedd Llywelyn where the battle took place had been charged on January 9th, 1959, by Adept Nixies Zero Zero One, the Cosmic Aspect of George King, during Operation Starlight. This mission, significantly, had commenced between himself and the Master Jesus four days before they combined again with Jesus delivering the first of The Twelve Blessings on July 27th, 1958. Then, on April 4th, six months after the Blessings had been completed and just one week before the Battle on Carnedd Llywelyn, George King gave his own Blessing to the Master Jesus as a fitting tribute and addition to these teachings.

Clearly, it had all been a brilliantly worked out strategy by these two interplanetary Masters in preparation for the impending battle with a buildup and interchange of spiritual power prior to the conflict taking place.

The relationship between George King and the Master Jesus evidently went back thousands of years, and feasibly far longer. He and the other two Adepts who accompanied him to Earth had not agreed with the brutal manner in which Jesus had allowed himself to die in a great karmic manipulation for the world; wrongly understood by Christianity that he came to take away the sins of the world. In a way he did but by the Law of Karma as previously discussed, humanity has a great debt to the Master Jesus which we have yet to realize, let alone repay.

As such, George King always found it difficult to speak about the Master Jesus without a great depth of emotion and reverence. It was also very typical of him to have tracked the evil magician behind the crucifixion through the centuries and to have arranged the situation in which he could bring about the transmutation of that entity. As George King explained it, when Jesus said from the cross "Forgive them for they know not what they do" he was implying that "they," the mob gathered before Pilate, had no idea of the evil interference brought about by "they," the black magicians, behind the scenes. It is an interesting perspective and casts a very different light on the crucifixion.

The other significant incident before George King sailed for New York took place on May 21st, one month after the Battle on Carnedd Llywelyn. His notoriety for taking the transmissions at London's Caxton Hall had attracted widespread interest such that it had reached the BBC. In a remarkable television program conducted live, he was interviewed by a psychiatrist in the presence of a Jungian psychiatrist and an astronomer both of whom later gave their own rather absurd opinions. Towards the end of the interview, George King was asked if he could go into trance under the glaring lights of the BBC studio to which he replied that he thought that he could.

Watching George King prepare himself to receive a transmission is unique in itself and the whole incident must make for one of the most unusual programs in their archives. The interviewer was then able to hold a two-way conversation with the Master Aetherius who, in the final question, was asked if he had any advice he would like to share. The Master Aetherius stated that he would and responded by saying, "If you are a Christian, then live the laws as laid down by Jesus. If you are a Buddhist, live the laws as given by Buddha. If you are a Hindu, then be the best Hindu. This procedure is the one true way for men of Earth to save themselves from their lower aspects."

Finally, watching George King come out of trance is either the finest piece of television acting or it is the genuine article. It is left for the viewer to decide. Either way, it brought George King to the attention of the masses and broadcast the message of the Cosmic Masters to an audience of millions.

Chapter 8

The Cosmic Plan

With the sole exception of George King and possibly his own mother, no one could have intuitively known or felt the global significance and implications of what was being unfurled by the Cosmic Masters through him at the time he sailed for America. He was more than a man with a hunch. He knew he was on a mission that was part of a much greater Cosmic Plan of which he had at least an inkling, and which had been foreseen and prepared for thousands of years before by some of the greatest minds in the solar system and even beyond.

Again, from the perspective of Divine Oneness, the destruction of Maldek together with the further evolution of the solar system needed to be accounted for in a way somewhat similar to how the body instinctively reacts to heal itself whenever a wound is incurred. It was not a process that would or even could be held up by the reckless actions and ignorance of terrestrials.

Moreover, in a startling transmission received by George King in May, 1958, it was revealed that the Mother Earth was due to die; in part as a result of being denied the energies she needed through the erection of the ionosphere following the fall of Lemuria, but also by mankind's renewed atomic experimentation during the Cold War. There had also been two very serious nuclear accidents just months earlier. The first of these was at Kyshtym in the Soviet Union in September, 1957, and the other just days later at Windscale in Northern England. Both poured radioactive particles into the atmosphere that threatened both mankind and the fine ecological balance of the Mother Earth. Incisive action needed to be taken and indeed

Maya Mire

was being taken by the Masters who not only cleared up much of the atomic radiation but also intensified their own actions.

This is the essence of this New World story. It has profound implications for every single one of us for what we are all now witnessing is an essential quickening of everything; a spiritual evolution on a planetary scale, and which most especially includes the Earth as the single most important aspect of this global change.

As such, it is imperative for all of us to become aware of this great Awakening and cooperate with it as it unfolds. We do not have to accept it—freewill remains a fundamental aspect of our present condition—but millions are being prompted by an inner, intuitive voice that recognizes that our civilization is facing profound danger; not just because of increasingly strained political, social, and environmental conditions but because our whole raison d'être as a species has become obscured and even lost. Something else much more fundamental and natural, akin to a great collective soul urge, needs to be and indeed is being birthed.

None of which is by chance. It is literally being orchestrated by great Cosmic Beings within and also far beyond our solar system. And yet none of us are bystanders; we are all essential parts of this change and the more conscious we each become of what is really taking place, on the scale of Laniakea, the more we can participate in the transformation.

Nor can we look at this story in a bubble. It is not solely about ourselves. We are each an intricate part of a Cosmic Whole, all working its way towards ever-expanding states of consciousness.

To assist in this global awakening, the Cosmic Masters sent one of their most valuable tools allowable within the karmic law. That is a giant spacecraft that has been orbiting Earth at regular intervals since May 28th, 1955. Known as "Satellite No. 3," it is a principal catalyst for this quickening through the enhancement of all selfless and spiritual actions by a factor of 3,000 times when in orbit, which is roughly a third of the year. It has been a driving force in the evolution of virtually every aspect of our lives since its presence was announced at the time by the Master Aetherius.

Six months earlier, in November, 1954, the Master Aetherius had made another important revelation to the world. It was published by The Aetherius Society in the book, *You Are Responsible!* The statement was no doubt made with the foreknowledge of Satellite No. 3 and the implications of this craft to Earth:

> *The evolution of mankind is now being speeded up, in order to reach a certain point within a certain time limit. Cooperate with the speeding up, help it, become the beings who speed this up and I promise you a million helpers. If you do, you will never regret any time you have spent in this wonderful way. There is so much for all of you to do, but so little time in which you can do it.*
>
> *...These are the teachings which we, from the Interplanetary Governmental Systems wish you to take, absorb, believe and act upon. Then we can make our next move, which will be free movement among you and direct help given in your schools, universities, hospitals and governments. If you go out of your way to reach up to us, we can and we will come out of our way down to you, but you must move! We cannot come unless you do this — this is the Law. We do not break the Law.*

As a consequence of this divine intervention we can either actively cooperate with this speeding up or else be moved aside. That is not to say in any aggressive way for the laws and demands of God are never aggressive even if they can at times seem that way. We are being molded in one form or another all within the Divine Law of Karma, and we can either assist in the evolutionary process of creation or else find ourselves being temporarily tossed and turned aside by this all-pervasive law, endlessly directing us towards conformity with Divine Will.

The orbiting of Satellite No. 3 is a major aspect of this Cosmic Plan for the salvation and enlightenment of mankind, as are the nineteen holy mountains that were charged by the Cosmic Masters during Operation Starlight, shining like jewels to provide us with another source of heightened spiritual energy. Similarly, the teachings that were given by Jesus in The Twelve Blessings provide us with a wholly new metaphysical and philosophical perspective of the living cosmos within which we exist, as well as a means to invoke a higher frequency of energy through the prayers.

In early 1961, as communications continued to be delivered through George King, the Intelligence in command of Satellite No. 3, Mars Sector 6, gave another set of profound cosmic teachings to stand alongside The Twelve Blessings. Known as "The Nine Freedoms," they outline our evolutionary journey within the solar system.

Beginning with *Bravery*—the vital need to recognize and act upon our inner voice of conscience, they take us through two other essential stages, *Love* and *Service*; all three of which together form a balanced path towards *Enlightenment*. However, unlike the traditional understanding of Nirvana as being our ultimate state, whether that is considered as Enlightenment or the higher experience of *Cosmic Consciousness*, The Nine Freedoms take us considerably further. With the attainment of Cosmic Consciousness, the consequence of having mastered the karmic lessons of Earth, we are no longer bound to this planet. As such, we undergo the mystic initiation of *Ascension* whereupon we can either remain upon Earth as an Ascended Master or go on to *Interplanetary Existence*. This exponential evolutionary progression eventually culminates with the extremely elevated experience cycle of *Saturnian Existence* before, ultimately, *Solar Existence* is attained in the Ninth Freedom.

It is a long upwards path and yet it is the one essential soul journey we are all making and always have been. There neither is, nor can there ever be, any avoidance of taking these steps towards Cosmic Oneness and ever-greater levels of expansion. All that there is and ever has been is a delay brought upon ourselves through acts of freewill as experienced in the mythological Garden of Eden and throughout our past.

Fundamentally, this timeless journey is leading us to ever-increasing levels of experience as the "This" of creation in order for us to increasingly know the no less exponential nature of "That," as in God. It is an ancient philosophy, beautifully illustrated in The Twelve Blessings and The Nine Freedoms. It is a comprehension and vision that now needs to be rekindled if we are to alter our collective course upon Earth and avoid any further nuclear destruction of ourselves and all life upon the surface of our world.

While these spiritual outlines of both our heritage and our destiny were being given, the work of George King was yet to really begin as other more critical aspects of this Cosmic Plan began to unfold.

In the telling of truth it can be hard not to be adamant about certain things. This book is simply to present these teachings and concepts in such a way that they can, hopefully, be understood.

Chapter 9

The Initiation of Earth

The experience on Carnedd Llywelyn in April, 1959, had clearly left George King in no doubt of his alternate status as an Adept, able to project from his body at will onto both higher and lower realms of existence. While this was nothing new to a yogi of this caliber, neither was it the type of rose-sniffing serenity ordinarily associated with this kind of so-called Master.

George King was different and profoundly serious, despite being largely dismissed by the sceptics as nothing other than a crank. But the few who gathered around him knew better, choosing to support him and his work with as much time, energy and finance as they each could provide. Thus, The Aetherius Society steadily continued to grow both in England and California.

George King's mission was slowly being revealed to him and he would need a handful of truly dedicated souls to assist him in this work. Besides, as terrestrials who had repeated the atomic destruction since Maldek, we were needed from a karmic point of view to help correct it.

Central to everything within the Cosmic Plan has been what the Masters called, "The Initiation of Earth."

Several of the transmissions being delivered through George King in the late 1950s and early '60s alluded to it as the fulcrum upon which all other changes would be made. It was to be the moment when the Logos of the planet was to be given a tremendous infusion of cosmic energy. These were the kind of energies that she had denied herself for more than 18,000,000 years and that, ordinarily, would have allowed her to attain a very different status in her own evolutionary journey.

Initiation is a rite of passage, something that has been earned and fully deserved as a major development in one's evolution. The Earth had done this through a divine act of sacrifice, not just by holding herself back to allow our incarnation upon her body but by limiting herself even further after the destruction of Lemuria and Atlantis. These both caused tremendous atomic fallout and the fracturing of her surface as well as the erection of the ionosphere. Thus was she denied essential life-sustaining energies for all of these subsequent years. It was akin to one of us not just being forced to hold our breath for an excessive length of time but to do so under tremendous duress at the same time. Relief was due in so far as she, as a planet, was dying while the Karmic Bell that brings an end to suffering had equally begun to toll.

In the early 1960s the buildup to the Initiation of Earth had already begun with a steady infusion of energies being given by the Cosmic Masters in phases known as "Operation One One One," each of which was fully reported through George King as it was undertaken. During these manipulations normally lasting from between 30 to 45 minutes in terrestrial time, stupendous amounts of spiritual energy were radiated from Satellite No. 3 through various cooperating Cosmic Agencies and directed into the Logos. These agencies included George King in his capacity as Adept Nixies Zero Zero One together with two other Adepts who had also taken on earthly physical bodies.

Without hearing these transmissions, it can be easy to dismiss all this as hooey, or "psycho-babble" as it is so described, but these audio tapes exist and they are profoundly real and serious; just as George King was intently serious, showing itself to all around him with an incredible vitality and mental force.

Other "Special Power Manipulations" also took place during the same period with some of those closest to George King such as Monique and Irène Noppe, Charles Abrahamson, Al Young and Ellie Jacobson being used as terrestrials through whom a tiny fraction of this energy was also transmitted. They each testified to the strong, cold sensation they could feel and the tremendous release once the operation was over. There was no doubting that a powerful force of energy was being sent through them as conduits even though it was just a miniscule amount compared to the Adepts and other agencies.

There was a momentum building towards some kind of tipping point in this unfolding Cosmic Plan. Nineteen mountains had been charged as great reservoirs of spiritual power for our own use. The Twelve Blessings and The Nine Freedoms had been given as outstanding cosmic teachings that defined the Divine Order of the universe and the essential metaphysical journey we are each making. The Twelve Blessings also gave a series of prayers that could elevate the mind to mystic states as well as transmit a stream of power outwards for the benefit of humanity, all of which was enhanced during the regular orbits of Satellite No. 3.

Each of these elements was a vital piece in this great plan that was clearly and plainly being erected as a superstructure to project humanity into the building of not just a New Age but, with the impending Initiation of Earth, upon a New World. A world as she would have been millions of years ago had it not been for the past folly of mankind; and a world within a solar system that no less would have been moving within the vast Milky Way at accelerating speed towards the immense heaven of Laniakea.

This is the journey we are all upon excluding no one and nothing and its energized reemergence, like the oncoming of a great cosmic storm, is driving a rush of wind before it that is now blowing upon us all.

As I wrote in the opening lines of Part I, *The Things I Knew Before I Was Born*, a planetary Awakening is now arising out of our profound slumber through the ages. It was a slumber darkened almost to blackness and with an unholy silence that had descended upon us after the fall of Maldek, millions of years ago in our time although a mere blinking of an eye in cosmic time; albeit an all-seeing Eye within the Mind of God.

Chapter 10

Operation Bluewater

While occasional phases of Operation One One One continued to take place in preparation for the ultimate and highly anticipated Primary Initiation of Earth, another Cosmic Mission was suddenly bestowed upon the already burdened shoulders of George King.

In a transmission delivered by the Master Aetherius in March, 1963, he was instructed to purchase a small vessel for this next operation that would be performed at sea off the Southern California coast. In addition, complex radionics apparatus would need to be built that could pick up high frequency energies relayed by the Cosmic Masters and convey these through an antenna system directly into a psychic center of the Mother Earth. The concept was similar in certain ways to Operation Starlight and Operation One One One in that higher frequencies of energy would again be injected from an outside source into the body of Earth.

As a yogi in his own right who had experienced the highest states of meditation, George King was very familiar with the psychic centers or "chakras," as they are known in the East, that we all have running along the spinal column. They are complex nerve vortices, such as the solar plexus and heart centers, through which subtle energy flows. However, in Operation Bluewater as this latest mission became known, the Cosmic Masters were dealing with a vortex of the planet.

It was a kind of thinking on a totally different wavelength to our common understanding, and yet the parallels embody a natural, intuitive sense. It is actually said by the yogis that we are each a unique replica of the galaxy, made up of trillions of cells each interrelated and all acting in a similar cosmic unison and symphony.

With regard to Operation Bluewater, our renewed atomic experiments had resulted in a buildup of radiation within the thermal belt of Earth causing a warp in the etheric path of the planet through space. As such, it was necessary to provide an infusion of higher energies into her body almost as a healing balm prior to the Initiation of Earth being performed. The mission would also help prevent a cataclysmic and overdue earthquake running along the San Andreas Fault line off the Pacific Coast of North America.

George King and his small team of helpers immediately pooled their modest funds and purchased a rather dilapidated vessel that they were soon able to make sufficiently seaworthy through their enthusiasm and tremendous hard work, both of which were manifested as a consequence of their deep appreciation for the importance of the upcoming mission and their unswerving commitment to the Cosmic Masters.

Operation Bluewater was performed in four separate phases between July, 1963, and November, 1964, over a psychic center of the Mother Earth approximately 14 miles off a location on the Southern California coastline known as Dana Point. During each of these phases, George King was instructed by the Cosmic Masters to steer the small boat through a series of complex maneuvers while a fine beam of energy was transmitted through the radionic apparatus onboard that his small team of helpers had built, and radiated out through an antenna that was trailed behind the vessel via a float. These energies penetrated hundreds of feet of seawater such that they could be drawn into the Mother Earth through the subtle interflow of energy naturally emanating to and from the planetary Logos through the psychic center.

Such an operation can, again, be beyond our rational minds to comprehend but when seen from a more intuitive and metaphysical perspective one can begin to appreciate the concept. To George King and his small team it was obvious, although each phase left him physically and mentally drained such were the intense demands of concentration placed upon him as he operated within two worlds throughout the roughly two-hour duration. This essential manipulation prior to The Primary Initiation of Earth was, like all else, carried out in obscurity without the kind of funding and attention it should rightfully have received had we been a more conscious race of humans.

And then, just before 10:00 p.m. Pacific Daylight Time on July 8th, 1964, George King was summoned by the Masters to induce a deep yogic samadhic trance. His close helpers knew exactly what to do having had considerable prior experience, and immediately took their positions at the tape recorders as well as at George King's side. However, none of them had anticipated that the moment had arrived for the great Cosmic Operation they had long been awaiting. Within minutes it was apparent that this was, finally, The Primary Initiation of Earth, and it was happening now!

George King did not know until about an hour later when, after 57 minutes, the transmission ended. An aspect of his mind suspected that this had been this pinnacle moment in the Earth's modern planetary history but he needed the others to tell him for sure before the tape was replayed such that he could know it for himself. Sometime after midnight he left the Society's headquarters on Crenshaw Boulevard in Hollywood and went for his nightly walk accompanied by one of his close helpers, Al Young.

He alone knew the significance of what had just transpired and of its future implications for all mankind. Everything had been changed. There would be no turning back of the clock. If anything, the clock was about to accelerate forward as earlier announced by the Master Aetherius. Little did humanity know either what had happened or what to expect. For the Logos of Earth, however, her ineffable flame had just been super-charged as she geared herself for a great and inevitable change.

Towards the end of the transmission, Mars Sector 6 who had coordinated the action, calmly stated, "This has been a very momentous occasion in the history of this Solar System." It was to mark the end of more than 18,000,000 years of withholding herself in sacrifice since Maldek, and the mark of a New Beginning in the Heavens as this cosmic infusion of energy is gradually released.

The transmission describing The Primary Initiation of Earth was written up by George King the following year in the greatest of all his books, *The Day The Gods Came*.

It had been a day the Gods came and would mark "A Bright New Dawn" for the Mother Earth and all those who are deemed ready by the karmic law. If there is a single date to signal the real beginning of this New Age, then that day has to be July the Eighth, 1964.

It was not the end of Operation Bluewater, however, with one more phase still being required. This took place on November 29th in the same manner as the previous three phases over the psychic center.

As for George King it was the closing of one pivotal chapter in the Cosmic Plan and the opening of another, albeit of an entirely different though no less staggering and momentous nature.

His work, inevitably, was to go on.

Chapter 11

The Alien

By the time Operation Bluewater was completed in late 1964, The Aetherius Society had continued to grow both in California and England as more people heard and accepted the cosmic transmissions being relayed through George King.

It was necessary to believe that these messages originated from intelligences other than George King himself, and that they were indeed coming from Masters inhabiting other worlds. While it took each person to determine these things to their own satisfaction, what, if anything, was a common factor in their decision was the depth of spiritual wisdom conveyed in the messages and the global significance of the Cosmic Missions combined with the profundity of both.

There was nothing trivial or petty about either. The concepts were vast and at the same time the transmissions were never pandering. One could only take them on board through rational realization and personal experience. Having done that, there was a call to roll up one's sleeves and become involved in the work to the extent that each person was able.

As important to weigh-up was the character and conduct of the spiritual leader, George King together with those around him. He was polite and formal in a traditional English sense, and intensely focused. This was balanced with a good humor and the direct, down-to-earth nature of a Yorkshireman who frequently wore a tweed jacket, drank copious cups of tea and who often had a dog near his side. As for his closest staff, they too were welcoming, unpretentious and deeply loyal to their Master. People were free to join and as free to leave. George King and those around him knew the work upon which they were engaged to be of the greatest importance to mankind and the planet and it had to go on, but no one was forced to sign up. Everyone was a volunteer with one or two employed as full-time staff on a stipend salary. As such the organization tended to attract individuals who carried a similar sense of spiritual mission without being fettered by any airs and graces. Had they had any, George King would have soon knocked it out of them or else they would have simply left. The Society had no room for "sight-seeing passengers" as the Master Aetherius once described them.

With a growing band of such dedicated followers, by June, 1965, the Society was able to move out of its rented premises on Crenshaw Boulevard into a sprawling but run-down property on a quiet street corner in Hollywood, close to the busy intersection known as Sunset and Vine. It comprised three buildings one of which would, once thoroughly renovated, make a more than suitable temple for the weekly services which the Society had been holding and for the lectures on metaphysical topics which George King frequently gave.

The other two buildings would provide accommodation for him and his closest followers together with offices and outbuildings for workshops. It was an ideal move forward and the outcome of all the previous hard work and dedication since George King came to the United States exactly six years earlier.

With Operation Starlight and Operation Bluewater behind them, together with scores of transmissions including the crowning glory of The Primary Initiation of Earth, they were gearing up for the future whatever that may hold. If they had planned their next move it would no doubt have been to build a Shape Power Temple on the new property to radiate spiritual power out to the world. But that, needless to say, was not to be.

In July, 1974, during one of the most outstanding public lectures George King ever delivered, entitled "The Cosmic Plan," he stated, "The Initiation of Earth precipitated many things..."

It was, if anything, an understatement, the outcome of which no ordinary human being could or would have ever foreseen or even imagined. For what was to come next in the summer of 1965 shortly after taking ownership of the new property was not only out of this world, it was out of this galaxy being totally "alien."

Again, one has to look at this whole story from a cosmic perspective. It is as impossible as it is daft for us to try and rationalize, let alone know, what else is going on within the vastness of infinite space light years away from our own small world. Simply put, we don't. Our knowledge and understanding are grossly ignorant of these things and yet, as per occult law, when we seek with an open mind and heart together with an honest sincerity and determination, the truth can be revealed. This is not to say we should ever abandon our own discernment, we should not. In fact, it is what will allow us to recognize truth once we encounter it.

At some point in our distant past, presumably long before Atlantis and Lemuria while we were still dealing with the smoldering after-effects of Maldek, an alien android took up residence in the lowest of the astral realms, or hells, around Earth. The stupendous energies radiated to the Logos during the Primary Initiation evidently disturbed this android from its ancient slumber.

Its presence was first detected in what was otherwise described as "a routine sortie" into these lower realms by the Adepts on May 30th, 1965. These three, including George King as Adept Number One, frequented these lower realms from time to time to perform some cleansing act such as in the Battle on Carnedd Llywelyn. The sorties were all communicated as they transpired through the voice of George King in his other capacity of "Primary Terrestrial Mental Channel," generally by the Master Aetherius who would give a graphic commentary of each action as it unfurled.

It was soon learned by the Cosmic Masters that this android was from an alien, hostile galaxy and its purpose for being dormant upon Earth was to await its instructions to strike within this part of the Milky Way. That moment had now clearly arrived and humanity stood by, albeit totally ignorant of the situation and about as useless.

Once more, it is easy at this point to throw in the book and discount such a story as utter nonsense but you would be rash and wrong to do so. Over the course of the following eight months the Three Adepts (who had now been made up to five given the severity of the situation) made 27 such sorties into the lower astral realms in combat with this alien android and its forces. Each of these actions was fully reported through George King in stunning detail by the Master Aetherius.

To say it goes beyond science fiction would be correct, but one can argue that truth is even stranger than fiction. These transmissions constitute the greatest occult, metaphysical and spiritual truths in the annals of our total cosmic history. They are recorded, they exist; and have only ever been played to select initiates within The Aetherius Society on very rare occasions. They are not, and will not be played to just anyone.

They were first played to such an audience in 1989, twenty-four years after most of the action had taken place such was George King's hesitancy to share such profound occult knowledge even among the Society's own proven members. Indeed, just prior to that initial playing, the Master Aetherius stated: "Tapes like these have never been played before on Earth—not even in the secret Retreats of The Great White Brotherhood!"

This was the Cosmic Plan as it was unfolding. It is this kind of truth and wisdom that lies far beyond the Mire of our own Maya; the ingrained ignorance that we have allowed to accumulate through our shared nonchalance and lethargy throughout the millennia. Yet it is precisely this kind of truth that will awaken us to a much greater cosmic reality. It is the kind of truth that will ultimately set us free. But it takes bravery and a spiritual determination to discover and ingest it.

The Adepts, with their staggering endurance and capability, eventually triumphed against the alien. On October 26th, 1965, five months after it was discovered, it was ejected from its lair in the lower astral realms. It was not killed because it was, we are told, un-killable. To throw it out of Earth and later out of this galaxy was all that could be done, albeit in the most brilliantly cunning and spiritual of actions.

The final end of The Alien Mission, as it is known, took place on January 22nd, 1966, one day before George King's 47th birthday. He was at the very height of his mental, psychic, and cosmic abilities.

Unfortunately for him, he needed to be, for there was another even greater karmic challenge soon to come.

Chapter 12

Gotha

This is the Cosmic Plan as we know it. This is the story that relates to each and every one of us as we look back through the dim and murky past beyond Atlantis and Lemuria to Maldek. Yet we must also look forward to the emerging and inevitable New Age; even a New World following the great fulcrum point of The Primary Initiation of Earth as it took place on July 8th, 1964.

This is the true narrative that humanity urgently and desperately needs in order to lift up our whole philosophical and spiritual vision and understanding of ourselves, and of our cosmic predicament in being here at all.

It is not, nor can it ever be, a false narrative. Life is too important, too precious, and too demanding. It is a profoundly true story in which we all are journeying. If there are heroes, and there are, they originate from beyond our world; all of them. Yet, in their unearthly advancement they do not look for glorification, for in the fullness of their own illumination there are even greater beings and, ultimately, only God worthy of such worship and adoration, all beautifully described and depicted by the Master Jesus in The Twelve Blessings.

This is the reality into which humanity and our world are now emerging. The outline related in these pages is, at best, an introduction to this greatest of all true stories. Not one of us can ever do it justice. The full picture can only be told in the great Akashic record within the ethers, but more than sufficient details can meanwhile be found within the archives of The Aetherius Society. This greatest of all earthly occult libraries contains more than 600 cosmic transmissions delivered through George King by the Cosmic Masters together with hundreds of mental transmissions also delivered by these same Masters. These were verbalized by him into a tape recorder as he telepathically received them without necessitating the extremely difficult induction of a samadhic trance as demanded in his former years as Primary Terrestrial Mental Channel.

In addition there are scores of lectures and addresses given by George King over a 43-year span on every kind of metaphysical subject. All of this spiritual knowledge can and needs to be weighed up and considered, alongside the ongoing Cosmic Missions and the simple practice of prayer as contained in The Twelve Blessings.

Those who feel so inclined will look to this path and take to it. It is merely my part to show this way forward and to speak from my own simple truth of having traveled this way throughout almost all of my adult life and, in my earlier days and George King's latter ones, at his side.

Following the completion of The Alien Mission in January, 1966, George King was ordered "off duty" and to rest by the Master Aetherius. The galactic challenge of The Alien Mission in his capacity of Adept Number One, the great strategist behind it all, had worn him to beyond the physical bone as it had with the mental and psychic strain which it similarly imposed. But, almost inevitably, that was not to be; and no less inevitably he rose to the next challenge which was requested of him with the same resolute determination as he had faced all the rest.

This request was made on February 13th, 1966, by a Master from another world, over 35,000 light years from our own towards the center of this galaxy. The system from which he had come was known by the pseudonym of "Gotha," and it was comprised of a few planets similar to our own of which just two were inhabited. They were an advanced race far beyond our capability, and they were profoundly spiritual in their outlook. The Gotha System, as we may call it, was under siege from the same race of aliens as had threatened this Earth though the inhabitants, with their spiritual perception, believed that the alien had as much right to their planet as they themselves. The Master who approached George King at his headquarters in Hollywood preferred to differ and, together with a handful of others, had called upon him to request the cooperation of the Five Adepts to intervene in the way that they had prevailed upon Earth. These "rebel" Gotha Masters had monitored the action of the Adepts during The Alien Mission and believed that by utilizing their skill and approach, they could free their own system from the same alien intelligence.

George King, true as always to his own nature and instincts, accepted the request and over the following twelve months the Adepts engaged in "The Gotha Mission" after convincing the authorities of that system that, should they allow the alien to inhabit their own planetary culture, it would leave other less advanced systems within the galaxy vulnerable to similar or even worse enslavement by the alien. In other words, it is one thing to surrender oneself to the enemy but not at the expense of others more defenseless. It was an important spiritual lesson for everyone.

The Gotha Mission was similarly reported by the Master Aetherius through George King in 16 phases over the following year with the Adepts once again prevailing in a final phase of super-galactic force. It was written up in July, 1967, by George King in *The Aetherius Society Newsletter* as "The Greatest Story Ever Told!"

The Gotha Mission tapes are even more rarely played than those of The Alien Mission. They exist in The Aetherius Society archives, just as they do in the Akashic record. They make anything and everything else of an occult and metaphysical nature appear as mere kid's play, not that this is their intention but simply as a matter of fact.

The New Age that is emerging upon Earth will embrace such a cosmic story and on such a grand scale, and we will accept it with the truth it requires. It simply awaits our own readiness to comprehend such vastness and to digest the full greatness of its veracity.

Chapter 13

Operation Sunbeam

The actions of the Adepts upon Gotha were not without significance for terrestrial man. Indeed, it is an intricate part of this cosmic story and our present condition upon Earth, even carrying over into our future.

Unlike terrestrials, the advanced Masters upon Gotha not only understood the all-pervasive karmic law but cooperate with it. As such, they knew that by this law they were indebted to the Five Adepts. It was karmically necessary to repay them for the freedom which the Adepts had won for their entire system from a similar enslavement as we would have been forced to endure upon our own world. The question was how to repay that debt to Intelligences who had no particular need of their own.

For those who knew George King, they understood that his mind never rested. He was constantly active, always pushing the karmic envelope at every turn and opportunity. It was one thing for Cosmic Masters to step in and assist humanity through the most transformative period in our total history, but it was "karmically necessary" for us to also step up to the plate. What could, and should we be doing in order to help dig ourselves out of the ignorance and apathy we have collectively sown over millions of years.

Both Operation Starlight and Operation Bluewater gave George King the inspiration and the tools that he sought. One was a supply of highly spiritualized energy that had been given to mankind; the other was a means of radiating such energy to the Logos of Earth. With his unique understanding of karma, George King knew that aside from anything the Adepts and other Cosmic Masters had done for the human race, nothing and nobody could compare to the sacrifice that had been made by the Mother Earth. Like a foster parent who had adopted a forlorn planetary race, she gave us all that we could ever need and, in the words of the Master Aetherius, even more than that.

Mankind may take such sacrifice for granted but karma cannot. The time would come when we would need to repay the Logos for all that she has given to us throughout the millions of years we have been here, such that we can gain the essential experience we need to set ourselves along the path of truth.

Operation Sunbeam was to be that means and it took George King to conceive of it. The concept was outstandingly simple; so simple that he was shocked that no other terrestrial Master had ever considered such an action before. His idea was to take some of the high frequency energy from the nineteen holy mountains charged in Operation Starlight and instead of using this energy for ourselves as it had been intended, it would be offered to the Logos of Earth through the psychic center he had learned about in Operation Bluewater.

The offer would be made as a token of thankfulness to the Logos for all that she had provided to humanity throughout the millennia. Even though the energy offered would only be a tiny fraction of what she is due, it would nonetheless be a gesture and, as such, would help tremendously in balancing the karmic debt of mankind.

It was while The Gotha Mission was playing out in the background throughout 1966 that George King set about Operation Sunbeam in earnest, describing in exact detail to Charles Abrahamson and Al Young the kind of radionic instruments that would be needed. One of the main aspects that had to be designed and built was a battery into which spiritual energy could not just be placed but held. Nothing like this had been seen on Earth at least since the days of Atlantis, and George King had no one he could call upon to help him. Once again, it all lay upon his shoulders.

As the months wore by, Charles and Al labored each night into the early hours of the morning building the apparatus George King had described. The battery would need to contain very finely ground crystal which George King took upon himself; an arduous and painstaking task that gave blisters after hours of grinding with a pestle and mortar. Gradually, the equipment came together and on September 24th, 1966, a small team climbed the nearby Mount Baldy, the tenth mountain to have been charged in Operation Starlight shortly after George King had arrived in Los Angeles seven years before.

Later that night he, with the aid of another Cosmic Master well-known to this Earth, invoked the energy from within the mountain and manipulated it into the crystalline battery that had been set up upon a tripod. It was straightforward yet complex at the same time; or, as George King would term it, astro-metaphysics.

Having the energy stored within the battery now meant giving it to the Logos of Earth. His team of helpers already had boating experience from Operation Bluewater and so, a week later and with the recent acquisition of another small vessel, the battery was taken out over a psychic center off the California coast at Goleta Point 100 miles north of Los Angeles that was linked via a major line of force with Dana Point, approximately 150 miles to the south. Using similar radionic apparatus to the earlier mission, the energy within the battery was drawn out and discharged into the body of the Mother Earth. Phase One of Operation Sunbeam had just been performed as a token repayment of high frequency spiritual energy to the Logos of the Mother Earth on behalf of all mankind.

Astro-metaphysics is perhaps a good way to describe it. It was certainly a science and spirituality beyond our common understanding. But then again, desperate times call for desperate measures. There was nothing especially desperate about Operation Sunbeam; it was simply an indication of George

King's otherworldly way of thinking and the determination, if not the genius, of a saint.

Among the hardest challenges which he faced was making Operation Sunbeam a sufficient karmic manipulation on behalf of the human race. After all, it was us who owed the planetary Logos, not George King or the Cosmic Masters. His initial solution was through the expedient of prayer by having a small picked team upon Mount Baldy for several hours prior to the charging of the battery to invoke streams of energy through the spiritual practice of The Twelve Blessings. However, this on its own was still not sufficient and George King knew it. To compensate for this shortfall of energy manipulation he had also arranged for members in Los Angeles and London and other centers to hold similar prayer sessions for a week in advance and several days after the battery had been charged.

While the principle was good, at least for Phase One of Operation Sunbeam, it would still provide a major challenge going forward. Some of his closest members were excellent in the practice of prayer but they were unable to invoke the kind of frequency this yogic science would require with energy being offered to the Logos of the planet. It was this aspect of Operation Sunbeam which continued to hold the biggest challenge for George King if further phases were to be performed, as he fully intended.

It was a problem that found an interesting and unexpected solution. Devising Operation Sunbeam and arranging for the building of the radionic apparatus had consumed much of George King's attention throughout the summer of 1966. But behind the scenes, in his capacity as Adept Nixies Zero Zero One, he had been engaged in evicting the alien forces from the system of Gotha. This led to two Masters from that system, including the one with whom he had had the first encounter, taking up residency upon the higher realms of Earth just weeks after Phase One of Operation Sunbeam had been performed.

This left him in a situation in which, on the one hand, he was faced with finding a workable modus operandi for Operation Sunbeam going forward, while on the other he had some of the Masters from Gotha offering their help in return for what he and the Adepts were performing upon their own world. George King was quick to join the two dots. Knowing that the Adepts did not need any help from the Gotha Masters, they could definitely assist with the future of Operation Sunbeam. It was an opportunity they immediately accepted with a further willingness to take whatever karma was necessary to enable Operation Sunbeam to continue into the future. It was a tremendous weight off George King's shoulders.

On October 15th George King received a cosmic transmission from the Gotha Master who had first approached him for help on February 13th. In the transmission this extremely evolved Master compared the "primitive squalor" of Earth and the conditions in which George King had to operate against the highly sophisticated scientific tools and spiritual environment which existed upon Gotha. To his mind, from a karmic point of view, what George King had demonstrated in Operation Sunbeam upon such a backward planet was a lesson that needed to be shared with other worlds throughout the galaxy.

This they did and in a follow-up transmission delivered by the Master Aetherius on December 18th, it was learned that Operation Sunbeam was now being spread like "a Cosmic snowball" throughout this galaxy as a lesson to more evolved races than ourselves who had otherwise considered themselves "not worthy" of making such an offering to the logoi of their own planets.

While George King was humbled and awed by this revelation, he had nonetheless found his solution for the invocation of suitable energies that would be needed for further phases of Operation Sunbeam.

Needless to say, that would have to wait as another even more pressing challenge was once again, if not inevitably, looming as the great Cosmic Plan for the salvation and enlightenment of mankind continued its world-changing momentum.

Chapter 14

Operation Karmalight

It was not by chance but by instinct and intuition that in his Introduction to *The Nine Freedoms*, written during 1963 in a place called Balboa Island near Dana Point where Operation Bluewater had been performed, George King included the statement: "... man stands today upon the verge of the most important happenings in his total history."

I reminded him of these words one morning in Santa Barbara more than 30 years later and I will never forget the gentle stare he gave back followed by the short, almost whispered response, "Of course."

The simple truth is that we are all now living through and living out the greatest happenings in our total history only for the most part we have failed to know it, let alone appreciate it.

That is the fundamental purpose of this book; to at least share this information. It is understood that for many the content will be mocked and ridiculed yet it has always taken just a few people to move humanity forward.

There are some wonderful quotes to consider in this context including that of the anthropologist Margaret Mead who famously said, "Never doubt that a small group of thoughtful, committed citizens can change the world; indeed, it's the only thing that ever has."

Similarly, the great Hindu Saint, Swami Vivekananda, pointed out, "Lies go with the wind. Truth can go against the wind."

And perhaps most applicable of all to this radical new way of cosmic thinking was the German philosopher, Arthur Schopenhauer, who wrote, "All truth passes through three stages. First, it is ridiculed. Second, it is violently opposed. Third, it is accepted as being self-evident."

That the cosmic philosophy of George King and The Aetherius Society has been ridiculed and opposed goes without saying; yet it has been self-evident to indigenous peoples since the beginning of time that the Mother Earth is a living intelligence and that "sky-people" exist. It is only Western civilization that has dismissed them through its own short-sighted cleverness and overdependence upon science.

We are all part of a Divine Cosmic Experience that can only be fully understood through an intuitive sense that requires most of all the quality of Love. It is an essence inherent within us all and yet it is, seemingly, the energy most lacking in our world today. We need to rekindle it together with a marveling at the very nature of our existence and that of the cosmos.

In 1984, the late dissident Soviet novelist, Alexander Solzhenitsyn wrote in an article published in *The London Times*, "the trouble with the West is that it has lost its consciousness of God."

I remember reading this at the time and totally agreeing with the sentiment, only thinking that, but for political correctness being mindful of the Soviet Union, he should have said "the world." Humanity is in peril, and we are in peril most of all because we have lost this divine sense of awe and mystery as to our origins and of our whole purpose for being here, and why.

George King and the teachings of the Cosmic Masters have given us this renewed philosophy and understanding, and they do so at a critical time in our history and evolution. It is imperative that we change, just as the Master Jesus stated in the Seventh Blessing to the Mother Earth, "She has not as yet demanded that you change—*or leave*."

It is not only ourselves that are under karmic pressure to change, the whole cosmos is being changed. It is the essential nature of the manifested universe. We are here to continuously evolve and to discover new and ever-higher levels of being and consciousness. It is a divine journey underpinned and surrounded by the energy and sensation of Love. To hearken back to Part I of this story, it is one of the great truths we all knew before we were born.

When seen and understood in this way, we can begin to open ourselves to all that has taken place since 1955, and especially during the decade of the 1960s behind the scenes of all our surface chaos.

On September 23rd, 1967, the Master Jesus and Saint Goo-Ling, an Ascended Master and prominent member of the Spiritual Hierarchy of Earth, gave two outstanding cosmic transmissions. They were published at the time by The Aetherius Society in a book entitled *The Three Saviours Are Here!* subtitled *The Transmutation of satan.*

The transmission from the Master Jesus begins:

Many centuries ago the Wise Ones looked into time and there They saw apparently inevitable results brought about by the fall of man. They conferred together, allowing the shining oil of sweet compassion to imbue Their negotiations. They took into consideration the deep Karmic implications of what was to come. Then turned They to Three devoted Beings and asked of These to give up the bliss of Their advanced Initiatory Status and take gross bodies, bound by Karma, held by the limitations of man and come and live and breathe and eat and pray and suffer among ye.

The Three Adepts spent no time in consideration.

Their Souls leapt within Them, filled with a compassion for a people who were helpless against the might which threatened to crush them, even as a great hammer crushes a lowly stone. And so it was They came and throughout the years that They have been with you, They have fought your greatest and most important battles.

Man, without the Three Adepts, you would have already been lost for a long, long time...

It is the same Three Adepts who have already been referenced in this book, with George King being Adept Number One. However, it was only at the outset of Operation Karmalight that we learned why he and his two comrades came to Earth under the extreme limitation which they did, and why they did at this time.

Again, when seen from the Divine Cosmic Whole and in the context of Maldek, Lemuria and Atlantis, we are a fallen race. If there is any doubt of this, then one slight cursory look at the present state of our world should be a stark reminder as to how fallen we are. It is not just our own existence that is at stake but that of our natural environment and planet, and all the myriads of life she sustains. We don't just need a new story, we need a new philosophical understanding and a New Vision in order to take us out of our dysfunction and chaos, and this has been given to us by the Cosmic Masters through George King.

Energy is energy. It has to go somewhere within the "allness of everything." The negative karma we have collectively created throughout our past has not simply disappeared, it has been sown. We have to reap that energy, that vibration, that consequence. In the interim, it has settled and accumulated most especially in the lower astral realms, or hells, of biblical proportion. We have created this energy vibration and added to it throughout our bloodthirsty past with our wars, our crime, our lies, our greed, our selfishness and wickedness in countless different ways, and most of all our inherent ignorance; all as a consequence of our choosing freewill so long ago.

Behind it all had grown a powerful intelligence we have termed "the devil," or "satan," and this intelligence had grown strong, able to manipulate much of the negative conditioning upon the surface of our planet. These are the foul denizens of evil encountered by the Adepts in all their previous sorties into these hells. Such hells and black magicians cannot be allowed to exist in the New World. A transmutation was needed and that time had come.

Another term for Operation Karmalight is "Armageddon." It is as steeped in myth and held together by the similar ties of truth as is the Garden of Eden. There is no such thing as absolute fiction. All have connections to truth; such is the nature of God and of being.

The foregoing transmission came at a time when George King was otherwise engaged in his work with Operation Sunbeam and his valiant attempts to still build a Shape Power Temple at the location in Hollywood, which had been given as an instruction from the Master Aetherius two years previously. But neither of these took precedence over Operation Karmalight. It was why he and the other two Adepts had come to Earth in the first place and he knew it utterly, as did that small band of humans who had stood by his side since he first settled in America.

One may well ask what was the difference between Operation Karmalight and the fight against the alien? The simple answer was one of karma. The alien was alien. The fight against the black magicians in the lower astral realms, most especially the one we had termed "satan," was man-made. We had created and fed this devil, this magician; and the hands of the Adepts were strictly tied as to how much outside help they could receive. It was, rightfully, our fight and if anyone could have tipped the balance and come to their aid, it should have been ourselves. But we were too embroiled in pop-culture and another of our own wars in Vietnam to heed this far greater fight taking place within the lower realms.

Operation Karmalight ran to 24 phases from October 26th, 1967, to February 24th, 1969. In the final action, satan was transmuted by Adept Nixies Zero Zero Six who had joined the Adepts Team. He is known throughout occult history as the Lord Babaji and is the political and Spiritual Head of the Spiritual Hierarchy of Earth. He has been on Earth in an ascended body since we came from Maldek, holding a karmic balance. He originates from Saturn, the most evolved and advanced planetary civilization within the solar system.

Most of the phases were, once again, fully described by the Master Aetherius as they took place and communicated through the voice of Primary Terrestrial Mental Channel, George King, who was seated in the newly-created Transmission Room at the American headquarters on Afton Place in Hollywood. However, unlike the previous two wars of the Adepts in the Alien and Gotha Missions, a few of the phases in Operation Karmalight were silent. We don't know why.

Unlike those two previous missions, this one was much closer to home. It was an earthly fight between the greatest forces for Good and the worst of the worst hells. As such, there was a price on George King's head and he had to be especially cautious and vigilant about everything. There was no margin for error and, as a consequence, it was an extremely fraught time at the American headquarters as well as in London where both staff teams were on constant "Red Alert." To relieve the pressure, George King would frequently announce a late-night party on the premises to throw off any hovering malignant entity; the idea being to confuse them by the apparent merrymaking. It was clever; it was subtle, as it all was deadly. The dark forces are cunning but thankfully not quite as cunning as the Adepts, all led by the chief strategist among them, Adept Nixies Zero Zero One.

Towards the end of Operation Karmalight, the Adepts were suddenly put under a further pressure to complete the mission within a certain time limit. They did so by several weeks even though the reason was never publicly given as to why this was so. It is possible to surmise that it might have been for an even greater Cosmic Initiation, that of the solar system. To know the answer we will have to read the Akashic record. Whatever it was, the Initiation of the Solar System was impending, as was the resumption of Operation Sunbeam which, since Operation Karmalight began, had been put on hold. George King's hands were full and fully tied until it was over.

The consequences, meanwhile, for ourselves were immense even though we had no idea. The strongest of chains binding humanity to the bonds of ignorance and darkness had been broken. As yet, the cost of this action has not been presented to us, but it will. It will have to be, by karmic law. The best we can do in the interim is to consider this story openly, not just with our mind but in the deepest recesses of our heart and soul, for in the transmission given at the outset of Operation Karmalight by Saint Goo-Ling on September 23rd, 1967, alongside the Master Jesus, he stated:

Be ye prepared to work for right — for this is the hour! The hour of the prophecies.
The hour of the turning point of evolution, or the hour of the defeat of all which is good and Holy upon Earth.
This is the hour.
The hour of Light or darkness.
The hour of Truth or lies.
THE HOUR WHEN THE FOUNDATION STONES CAN BE LAID FOR THE NEW AGE OR NEVER CAN IT BE BUILT BY MAN UPON THIS PLANET.
This is the crossroad of evolution. It is the beginning of greatness, or the beginning of darkness.
It is the hour of Light, or a more stifling blackness than you have ever known before.
You stand as helpless children in this hour.
It is the hour when the Karmic book is written for each and every one of you. When the Searchers look deep into your heart, your

Soul and your environment and make Their judgment—yes judgment—accordingly.

It is the hour of supreme triumph of all that is Glorious, or defeat of the best. The battlefield has been chosen. The armies are taking their terrible position.

Indeed, was George King right when he wrote in his Introduction to *The Nine Freedoms* four years earlier, "... man stands today upon the verge of the most important happenings in his total history."

Operation Karmalight was just one of those happenings and one of the most important, for all of us.

George King in the Transmission Room at the American headquarters

Chapter 15

After the Wars

Over the course of the summer months of 2006 and 2008 I had the opportunity to interview Charles Abrahamson and his wife, Ellie, about the 1960s. They had both, especially Charles, hardly left the side of George King throughout these years, not even for much of a so-called "vacation" which was a rarely used word and an even rarer practice. Indeed, it was not until the following decade that Charles and Ellie were even able to marry such was the intensity of life at the American headquarters of The Aetherius Society throughout this entire period.

The decade had begun while Operation Starlight was only half finished in America with two more mountains still waiting to be charged. Charles and Irène had accompanied George King on some of these and, in Monique's case, all of them. The years 1963 and 1964 had primarily engaged them with Operation Bluewater together with the numerous Special Power Transmissions and phases of Operation One One One, culminating with The Primary Initiation of Earth on July 8th, 1964.

Then, in quick succession, came The Alien Mission, The Gotha Mission and Operation Karmalight that had exacted the most extreme pressure on George King and, by extension, on all of his staff. It was during The Alien Mission that, as Charles recalled, "We stopped calling him George." Instead, "Dr. King" became the term most commonly used by his staff and members. He had simply become too far above them in occult stature and presence that to be as familiar as to use his first name just seemed wrong.

The only one who did still call him George was Monique who was the closest to him of all. Simply put, she loved him; although, as did they all. It was hard not to love him. He was just so exceptional, so unusual, so brave and otherworldly; and yet in so many other ways, so down-to-earth and practical; and perhaps most of all, so humble, without ego or fanfare. He knew he had a job to do and he was doing it when nobody else on the planet could. It was as simple as that so he just got on with it and did it in the only way he knew how, which was superbly. And when he could kick back then he did so but only for a short while. His guard could never be fully let down and never was, not even to his dying day.

On top of all these otherworldly demands, George King had chosen to add Operation Sunbeam. It was his mission and not even the Master Aetherius had considered it although, to be fair, he knew George King both as a man and as an Adept and was doubtless one of the Wise Ones who had "looked into time" and called upon him as one of the Three Adepts to come to Terra. As such, he never put anything past George King who, many years later, he referred to as, "My Star Pupil, and always has been, even before he came among you."

Meanwhile, the cosmic transmissions continued to come through, all of which needed to be transcribed with many of them being published in *The Aetherius Society Newsletter*. This came out more or less monthly in lengthy editions containing all kinds of information and updates about the work going on throughout the Society in several different locations. The journal was entirely created upon the property with George King sometimes operating the printing press.

By the end of the decade George King was at his absolute peak, turning 50 just a month before Operation Karmalight came to an end. He was not only a proven Master, he was a Cosmic Adept and he brimmed with energy and vitality. In that sense, he could be difficult to be around, and if your heart was not entirely in the organization and the rigorous demands that were exacted then the chances were that you would not stay, though most did.

The end of Operation Karmalight could, in a way, be seen as a time to relax a little. Charles and Ellie were married the following year and, one year after that, so were George and Monique with Charles conducting the ceremony. They had always been close with Monique acting as his main secretary, cook, healer and confidante. She was the one who sat beside him in the Transmission Room and, together with another staff member, would bring him back to earth following each of the tremendously rigorous ordeals of samadhic trance. Besides a table and chair, magenta lighting and three microphones, the one other main feature in this sound-proofed room was a bed onto which George King would collapse after coming out of trance. The body had gone cold as all the energy and focus were placed upon the highest chakras in order to bring through the transmission. Monique, more than anyone, knew how he was suffering for this alien race of humans and cared for him deeply. That having been said, despite their closeness, the marriage was entirely celibate. George King, first and foremost, was a yogi adept. Sex was for procreation, not pleasure, and children were never on the forecast for either of them.

At the very end of the decade, on December 28th, 1969, the Master Aetherius delivered one more transmission for the year and the decade. It is perhaps one reason, if not the main one, as to why Operation Karmalight had a time limit placed upon it much earlier that year.

It was learned during the transmission that over the past several months the solar system had received an Initiation affecting all the planets other than Earth which was shielded. Everything had been heightened onto another frequency as the natural course of evolution took its place. Mankind's destruction of Maldek had slowed the system down. This had now, largely, been rectified with the Initiation of Earth five years earlier, the eviction of the alien and the cleansing of the worst aspects of the lower astral realms in Operation Karmalight. It was time for the solar system to move on, towards where it should have been and would have been were it not for the folly of mankind more than 18,000,000 years before.

In his remarks, the Master Aetherius pointed out that mankind would now be able to land his rudimentary craft on other bodies within the solar system, something previously forbidden. The United States that year went to the Moon. No life was detected, but then again everything had been vibrated onto another level of frequency. Life does indeed go on, for all of us on all levels. Besides, Laniakea and evolution cannot wait indefinitely.

Chapter 16

The 1970s

It could be said that with the coming new decade most of the essential work of the Adepts and George King was over. Most importantly, Operation Karmalight, the primary reason they came, was for the most part over. As it turned out, neither Karmalight nor The Alien Mission were entirely over. There was still some mopping up to do in what was termed the "Aftermath" of both missions.

Besides the great fulcrum of the Initiation of Earth on July 8th, 1964, there had been one other anticipated cosmic event that George King and his close helpers had cautiously awaited. It was known that at some indeterminable time, an avatar would come openly to Earth. This prophesy had been made to George King on November 23rd, 1958, upon a hilltop known as "Brown Willy" in southwest England immediately after this remote location became the second mountain charged in Operation Starlight. It was unknown when that much prophesied time might be although the word used by the Cosmic Intelligence was that it would be "shortly." Shortly in cosmic terms can have a very different connotation to our own, with the inference that the circumstances of his coming would be somewhat dependent upon the karma of the human race.

This situation remains fluid to this present day but one thing that did become known was that the Adepts' success in Operation Karmalight would mean that the next Master would not need to expend his own precious energy facing the same challenge from the lower astral realms. Instead, he would be able to focus his full attention on preparing humanity for the great spiritual change which is to come.

Meanwhile, George King could now turn his attention to advancing Operation Sunbeam by finding other psychic centers which could be used inland rather than upon the dangerous waters of the Pacific Ocean. With the two Masters from Gotha capable of invoking the frequency of energy that would be needed, his new concern was to devise a radionic system that could pick up the energies they invoked upon charged mountains besides Mount Baldy which, at over 9,000 feet, was high and hard to climb, especially when carrying weighty, precious equipment. This new apparatus all needed to be built and successfully tested which it was. After considerable research, another psychic center was found by George King at Lake Powell on the Arizona–Utah border in May, 1972, that would be receptive to the battery discharges and far easier to navigate in a small boat.

Three months later, while sitting in his private apartment above the European headquarters on the Fulham Road in London, George King received an out-of-the-blue contact from an extremely elevated Cosmic Intelligence who went by the strange name of "Questing." This entity graphically illustrated to George King how the potency of Operation Sunbeam could be doubled if he was able to extend the mission to the British Isles. This would entail a metaphysical survey of the main island, possibly both, which would require considerable forethought and planning since trying to find a suitable psychic center within such a wide area was rather like looking for a needle in a field of haystacks.

This contact had come when George King was already looking to adapt the concept of Operation Sunbeam in such a way that it would utilize members of The Aetherius Society and the general public in a karmic manipulation of their own. With his deep understanding of karma, he knew how necessary it is for humanity to be engaged in selfless spiritual action, not just for the sake of the action but in the entire mindset behind it.

In a way, the whole principle of creation is enacted in selfless service all borne out of the knowledge of Oneness which, in itself, is a fully conscious realization of Love. It is the ultimate essence of "God," with God being the timeless Server of All. It is a vital lesson for humanity to grasp, and indeed needs to become the primary motivation of us all. It is the fruition of "the way" as depicted in Taoist philosophy, and is essential in reversing the stunted and unnatural position of our present selfishness and greed.

With Questing's prompting still ringing in his ears, George King returned to Britain the following summer to inaugurate this other mission which he called "Operation Prayer Power." It relied upon the invocation of spiritual energy through dynamic prayer and mantra which would again be directed into a crystalline battery, as used in Operation Sunbeam. However, instead of this energy being offered to the Logos of Earth, which it was far too weak to do, it would be radiated in a very concentrated stream for the relief of human suffering in times of emergency, such as after an earthquake or other natural disaster.

The inauguration took place on June 30th, 1973, upon Holdstone Down in Devonshire, the original mountain charged fifteen years before in Operation Starlight by the Master Jesus, and using the prayers this Master had given in The Twelve Blessings.

Three months later, now back in the United States, on September 23rd the mission was inaugurated in the Americas on a beach at the side of the psychic center at Lake Powell with members of The Aetherius Society coming from across the United States and Canada. The single most important tenet in George King's yogic approach was Service, or "Karma Yoga," and he was endlessly seeking ways in which humanity can serve the greater whole whether it is the Logos of the planet, mankind, or an individual.

In the summer of 1974, with Operation Prayer Power now established on two continents and with several discharges of the energy having already been made—including to the Turkish–Cypriot crisis which resulted in a sudden ceasefire of hostilities, George King turned his attention to making a survey of Britain in a preliminary attempt to locate a psychic center of the Mother Earth on the earlier promptings of Questing.

Finding nothing but having commenced the process with the purchase of a boat, he returned to Britain two years later in May, 1976, to continue his search. He knew, based upon the visualization given by Questing, that such a situation was possible; it just required someone like himself with exceptional occult and psychic abilities to pull it off. Moreover, from a karmic point of view, the answer couldn't just be shown to him. He was acting on behalf of terrestrials and for the full karmic potency of the mission to be realized it required someone in a terrestrial body to carry out the task. Indeed, this had been the pattern from the beginning with all of the Cosmic Missions he had been required to perform.

In the event, he found two psychic centers a little over a month later although only one of which could be practicably used. That was over Loch Ness in Scotland, the other being in the Bristol Channel at sea. Loch Ness, he was to discover after hundreds of hours of research upon its surface, was the fifth most significant psychic center on the planet.

Meanwhile, in the previous year, 1975, Mars Sector 6 had agreed to George King's request for Satellite No. 3 to manipulate the Operation Prayer Power energy when the craft was in orbit of Earth. This energy amount had steadily been building with weekly charging sessions at the Society's main centers in Britain and the United States. With the mission now being touched by the Cosmic Masters it took on an even greater karmic potency.

In fact, Satellite No. 3 had been manipulating spiritual energy through radionic apparatus devised by George King since the late 1950s. The original instrumentation housed in London was rudimentary to say the least but it was sufficient enough for the Masters to pass a beam of energy through it making this even more accessible to mankind. Meanwhile, in Los Angeles, the apparatus he had used in Operation Bluewater to receive and transmit spiritual energy was adapted such that it could also radiate a beam of energy from Satellite No. 3 during the times it was in orbit. This equipment was replaced in 1969 with a more portable model, termed a "Spiritual Energy Radiator," and which had been used for the discharge of the battery in Operation Sunbeam. A replica was built in 1971 and shipped over to London to replace and upgrade their original model, the main components of which were affectionately named "Gertie" and "Gertina" by their operators.

The radiation of energies from Satellite No. 3 through the Spiritual Energy Radiators in Los Angeles and London became known as "Operation Space Power" and exists to this present day, only now with five Spiritual Energy Radiators on the air for several hours each day during every Magnetization Period, or "Spiritual Push," when Satellite No. 3 is in orbit.

With the steady development of these Cosmic Missions throughout the 1970s, The Aetherius Society continued to grow, at least in English speaking countries. Meanwhile, in his cosmic aspect as Adept Number One, George King was still very active on the other realms. Together with the Adepts he was devising a remarkable way to make Operation Sunbeam even stronger, not for the sake of it but for the sake of the Mother Earth who still needed as much potent spiritual energy as the mission could provide.

This commitment to spiritual service is the essence of the New Age mentality which humanity has to adopt if we are to truly live to our highest good. We need to become conscious of our divine heritage recognizing that life is infinite beyond the temporary apparition of death. We are here to advance and evolve and to do, in the words of the Master Jesus, "even greater things" than even he had done. In short, we are not here to suffer but to grow and expand. This has been the principal gist of George King's message and of the Cosmic Masters who ever spoke through him.

They are not remote, as the Master Aetherius once put it, but await our own stepping forward beyond the limitations and ignorance we have imposed upon ourselves for millennia. This was the message being put out by George King and the organization he had founded, and those who were seeking such a path and inspiration to follow were now finding it.

On September 23rd, 1979, in the penultimate cosmic transmission George King was to receive, notification was given that Operation Prayer Power was being inaugurated on "Level 4," one of the six higher realms above this physical plane with 60,000 people attending the opening session. Inevitably, and according to occult protocol, George King was invited to take part as the guest of honor. He projected onto Level 4 and initiated the mission with an invocation of spiritual energy into the battery. It was all described in wonderful detail by the Master Aetherius and was further revealing about this unusual "human" intelligence and the respect in which he is held on the higher realms of Earth.

This is what the dawning of the Age of Aquarius really looks like in the raw. It is to move beyond the Maya Mire of our ignorance and weakness and see things as they truly are through a cosmic lens of Spiritual Oneness.

Chapter 17

The Final Decades

If there was any winding down with George King when he turned 60 in January, 1979, it was not apparent. He was far from done with improving Operation Sunbeam which he was intent on setting up for the future. Throughout the past decade it had been the major focus of his attention but George King still did not have it down to his complete satisfaction. Now, thirteen years after Phase One had been performed with 50 phases under his belt, he had spent the past several years, and especially since the contact by Questing, seeking to perfect it.

In a visit to the Lords of the Flame, the most evolved intelligences existing on the planet, in January, 1972, he had been informed that Operation Sunbeam was more important to the world than any other operation being performed on Earth by any organization or even country. It was a massive statement that, taken on its own, seems ridiculous. But when seen as all work needs to be seen from a cosmic perspective, it can be understood.

Humanity is in debt to a great Cosmic Goddess who, for millions of years, has provided us with the greatest gift that we could ever have, that of karmic experience. At the end of everything, that is all that truly matters; not wealth, not fame, not any kind of singular importance. All shall be washed away in the fullness, or even shortness, of time. Evolution is the name of the game and the Earth has provided that for each of us.

The very concept of humanity giving back to the planetary Logos as a gesture of thankfulness and appreciation goes to the very root of the whole ecology movement which, interestingly, sprang up just months after Operation Sunbeam was inaugurated.

Appreciation through Realization is the path to true greatness, and Operation Sunbeam had set us down that path. It is why the Gotha Masters took the mission to the galaxy. If humans could make this appreciation, albeit just as a "token" and amid their "primitive squalor," then so could any planetary race. George King fully understood this and so it was important for him to make it as perfect as possible.

By June of 1979 he had performed the first phase of what he termed "Plan B" of Operation Sunbeam in which the spiritual energies invoked by the Gotha Masters, who now numbered three, could be relayed through our radionic apparatus directly into a psychic center. It was no longer necessary to temporarily hold the energy in a battery awaiting discharge by ourselves. It was a major breakthrough in helping to ensure the success of the mission into the future, but for George King it was still not enough.

That is why over the previous four or five years he had been working with his fellow Adepts to extend the source of spiritual energy beyond the holy mountains that had been charged in Operation Starlight.

Over five days in early March, 1980, four modules were placed by the Adepts on the physical realms of Saturn, Jupiter, Venus and Neptune. That it had taken them this length of time to execute this operation demonstrates its highly advanced and complex nature. However, it still awaited a further component to make it functional. This took place the following year on George King's 62nd birthday, January 23rd, 1981, with the placing of a satellite known as A1 into orbit, "A" presumably standing for Adepts.

The mission was termed "Operation Space Magic" and it enabled the Gotha Masters, or even the Adepts themselves, to draw energy from each of these planets and offer this to the Logos of Earth in addition to the energies contained within the holy mountains. These were vital cosmic energies which she had been denied since the erection of the ionosphere. What is more, since the Initiation of the Solar System had taken place more than a decade before, these energies were of the higher frequency from which she, herself, had been further denied due to the shielding of Earth during that Initiation for our sake.

A few weeks after the placement of Satellite A1, George King received his very last cosmic transmission in March, 1981. It was very different than the 600 that had gone before over the previous 27 years and it marked a fitting culmination. It was the giving of Cosmic Awards by agencies throughout this solar system, primarily to the Adepts for all that they had achieved. Significantly, it also recognized Operation Sunbeam and George King, both essential in the overall Cosmic Plan for the salvation and enlightenment of mankind upon Terra.

It was a crowning moment that was not without its repercussions later that same year when, on September 26th, George King was crowned as a prince in a ceremony that took place in St. George's Chapel in Hanover Square, London. Although this was not performed by any recognized royal house, it nonetheless followed another great metaphysical law: *As above so below.* It was karmically necessary for mankind to recognize and thank George King even if it meant doing so through less well-known and established channels.

The overall karma that George King and Operation Sunbeam had woven for the world made it possible for even further cosmic intervention, coming from the highest planetary sources within the solar system. This became known as "The Saturn Mission" and was to be performed under the auspices of the Lords of Saturn, the most evolved Masters in our system and the Seat of Interplanetary Parliament.

Its purpose was for World Peace and Devic Stabilization, and it followed the same principles as established for both Operation Sunbeam and Operation Prayer Power. Literally, to place energy into a battery and release it to another area of need. In this instance the energy would be invoked by the Adepts and released over one of the main psychic centers used in Operation Sunbeam, namely Lake Powell in Utah and Loch Ness in Scotland. In this process the very high frequency energies would intermingle with the natural energies flowing from these psychic centers and be offered to the Higher Devic Kingdom.

The Western term for "devas" would be nature spirits and all of creation is governed by them. They are responsive to the energy that is made available to them and, as such, by the karmic law, we reap what we have sown. This applies most especially to weather patterns but also earthquakes and other, so-called, "natural disasters." They are natural in that they respond to the energy mankind collectively puts out, while the disaster is merely a consequence to the frequency of energy we have provided.

The Saturn Mission would help to counterbalance that with its infusion of tremendously beneficial energy invoked by the great Adepts, very likely from the other planets using Satellite A1 which they had placed in orbit earlier that year. A secondary consequence would be the aiding of world peace.

It was clearly known and foreseen by the Cosmic Masters that this period through which we are now living would be a time of tremendous upheaval and challenge. The best and only real antidote is the outpouring of spiritual energy. It is the reason behind everything George King, the Adepts and the Cosmic Masters have done both now and throughout our past. They cannot, however, do all the work for us. We have to be the ones who utilize this higher frequency of energy such as that offered by Satellite No. 3, as well as the ones invoking it from the holy mountains and through our own spiritual practice, such as The Twelve Blessings.

Phase One of The Saturn Mission took place over the psychic center at Loch Ness in September, 1981. Further phases, together with regular phases of Operation Sunbeam, were performed on an ongoing basis throughout the remainder of the decade and into the 1990s. Both missions have continued into the present day.

That was always the intention for Operation Sunbeam but unexpected for The Saturn Mission which was performed by the Adepts with George King piloting a boat during the discharge. Each phase of this mission consists of three sub-phases, each performed in the same way and each dependent on the prevailing weather conditions since it is necessary to keep the on-board battery sufficiently stable so that the energies can be withdrawn by the Adepts in a space vessel of their own hovering above. Again, like all of the Cosmic Missions, the principle is simple and seemingly straightforward, but making the simple happen can sometimes be complex in itself.

By the end of the decade George King was looking even more to the future. He had turned 70 years of age in 1989 and his health was becoming the worse for wear. The past 35 years had placed immeasurable strain upon his shoulders, as it had in different ways for the likes of Monique, Charles, Irène, Al and others. They had all been in it, literally, for the long haul. It had been a unique and exceptional journey, and utterly life-changing for the world. It is why others, such as myself, have come into the organization to help not just with the work they all set up and left in our care but to help carry it forward.

With his eye now firmly upon the future after his demise, George King summoned an International Directors meeting in August, 1990, held in the temple at the American headquarters in Hollywood. I had only recently arrived from England and was working in the adjacent office as Lady Monique's assistant.

During the meeting the question arose about another mission George King had devised but which was still not being performed. That was Operation Earth Light which had roots going back to Operation Sunbeam and Operation Prayer Power.

Its function was similar to The Saturn Mission except that the radionics apparatus, which had not at that time been built, was to help release the energies held by the Logos of Earth following her Primary Initiation. It was, in effect, applying a homeopathic dose of these stupendous forces to the Devic Kingdom and ourselves, essentially to help prepare us for the Great Change that is to come.

Clearly, it was another massive consideration for George King to take on board, let alone perform with his own ailing health and limited staff and resources. His hands and those of The Aetherius Society were already more or less full. And yet the mission needed to be performed. It was too important simply to ignore, and anything of a cosmic nature, George King could never ignore.

Thus it was wisely decided during these meetings to offer the mission to the Lord Babaji and the Spiritual Hierarchy of Earth for them to perform, assuming they would accept the offer which they did with immense respect and appreciation.

Years before, in a mental transmission George King had received from the Master Aetherius when discussing Operation Earth Light, he had been told not to concern himself about it at that time and that "others will follow." It was doubtless the Master Aetherius' all-seeing psychic eye that had foreseen the eventuality which played out. Besides, the Ascended Masters could do the mission the justice it both required and deserved, and within a few weeks the apparatus which George King had devised seventeen years earlier was copied and being tested by these Masters.

On November 11th, 1990, three months after the mission had been offered to the Spiritual Hierarchy, Phase One of Operation Earth Light officially went "on the air." George King was at Lake Powell at the time, and when he was informed of this inauguration by the Lord Babaji he found himself walking along the shore "crying like a baby."

It showed his human heart together with his cosmic appreciation. His own unique sacrifice and hard work were continuing to bear fruit in the fullness of God's Plan for humanity upon Earth.

And then, on January 17th, 1994, the Northridge earthquake struck Los Angeles County and George King was forced to take refuge in his private home in Santa Barbara, his own residence in Hollywood at the headquarters having been jolted off its foundations. This was covered in Part I of this story and where I came more into it. However, it was still not the end of George King's involvement with the Cosmic Missions. There was more, much more, yet to come.

The first of these was the surprise addition of Operation Power Light which had actually begun the previous year. It was a remarkable mission in at least one way and similar to all the rest in another. That was again using the principle — the great Cosmic Principle — of taking energy from a higher source and directing it to an area or situation of greater need, in this case for World Healing and Upliftment. It utilized spiritual energy taken from a reserve held by the Cosmic Masters that had originally passed through our Spiritual Energy Radiators during the orbits of Satellite No. 3 but had not been used by mankind and was therefore recalled to avoid resonance. During the first eleven phases an additional stream of energy was passed through George King, but as the mission wore on it became more complex with energy also being drawn from several of the holy mountains. It simply became too powerful to be passed through George King who, by the mid-1990s, was increasingly frail. However, that did not matter. Indeed, it was the mere fact of his cooperation that enabled the mission to be performed at all, never mind extended. All he needed to do was to be somewhere, either in his own home, in the Society's temple or at some outside location of his choosing.

It again was very simple in its concept and yet it was a beautifully touching gesture to the man and yogi adept the Cosmic Masters had all come to revere and indeed love. It was in so many ways the virtual opposite of his first Cosmic Mission he was tasked to perform, that of Operation Starlight which had extracted extreme hardship and excruciating pain from George King, leaving him at the doorstep of death on more than one occasion.

The rigors and demands of Operation Sunbeam had also taken their toll, not to mention the missions of the Adepts in the hells and upon Gotha; and the more than 600 cosmic transmissions he had received. He had given his life's blood to his cause, and his cause was outstandingly holy.

As such, Operation Power Light was different with an increasing array of Cosmic Intelligences virtually coming to salute him in the final chapter of his life. Being George King, it had to have a beneficial element which of course it did in radiating another potent stream of spiritual energy to the world for suffering humanity. Initially he found the phases a little strange and he would often need to lie down once they were over. As someone who shared his home and proximity when many of the phases were being performed, I found there was always a lightness of energy that was tangible and highly elevating to experience. Altogether 44 phases of Operation Power Light were performed, the first being on March 18th, 1993, beside a mountain lake north of Santa Barbara and the final one taking place in his own home in May, 1996.

However, it was still not quite the end with yet another twist in Operation Sunbeam. This occurred without warning for George King who, so it seemed, the Masters did not wish to disturb or trouble. All the love and karma he had poured into his mission had allowed it to take on even greater spiritual power and influence for the world. Its new modus operandi, which the Masters termed "Plan K" in his honor, enabled a greater quantity of energy to be manipulated during each phase and opened up other psychic centers of the Mother Earth that could now also be utilized during the mission. This included both the original centers off the coast of Southern California at Dana Point and Goleta Point as well as two new centers, one within the Arctic Circle and highly significant to the planet, and the other within Lake Tanganyika in East Africa. A new format was worked out whereby a total of 16 phases would be performed each year by trained initiates within The Aetherius Society.

Lastly, in November, 1994, The Saturn Mission was offered to George King for The Aetherius Society to take into the future. After careful consideration due to the highly elevated nature of the mission and the karma involved, he eventually accepted and a modus operandi was carefully devised by senior personnel within the organization who were familiar with the performance of these sacred missions. In 1996 this plan was shown to the Master Aetherius for his approval, which he gave.

The final dots and crosses of George King's life were each being carefully marked off. Only he and the Master Aetherius really understood it and its implications for mankind's future. It will take lifetimes for us to unpack and centuries before we can truly appreciate what it all was about.

At 4:48 a.m. on Saturday, July 12th, 1997, he took his last breath. I had been at his side holding his hand for the previous few hours. He told me he was dying which I knew; however, I felt him too delicate in that critical time to leave on his own. In fact, I felt it necessary and important not to leave him alone even for a moment such that I could help him through the difficult process. He understood, perhaps more than we ever will, what it meant to the world for him to leave it.

Then, when he became very settled shortly before 4:00 a.m., I summoned Brian in the neighboring room who awoke Richard and the three of us nursed him through the final hour. In Los

Angeles at the headquarters, the Spiritual Energy Radiator had been activated through which the Cosmic Masters directed their energy. Finally, the end had come.

A few hours later the paramedics arrived to remove the body. It was over. Not just the passing of a life but the ending of an era and the start of a whole new world. It is now just a matter of time before that, too, becomes a Whole New World.

Later that day I called my parents in England to let them know the Master had died. It had been expected. The call was not answered so I presumed, rightly, that they had gone away for the weekend. When I reached them again the next day on their Sunday evening, I was told that they had been to Combe Martin of all places, the village beside Holdstone Down and more than 100 miles from their own home, much of it through winding country roads. After a pause, my mother asked me what time he had died. I replied that it was at about quarter to one on their Saturday lunchtime. My mother thought for a moment before saying, "Good heavens! Do you know it was exactly at that time that we were driving by Holdstone Down and I said to your father, 'Stop the car, I want to get out.'" And for the first and only time in my mother's life, she went onto the mountain that had meant so much to the Master, and where I had first seen him almost exactly 12 years before, to say a prayer for the soul of George King.

Little did she know that 6,000 miles away he was passing over at that exact same moment while I knelt at his side holding his right hand letting him go.

Indeed does God work in mysterious ways His wonders to perform.

George King's private home in Santa Barbara, California

Afterword

This short book is not an attempt to encapsulate everything that has occurred during the life of George King as Primary Terrestrial Mental Channel, Adept Number One, and simply as himself, the man. It cannot be and besides it would be superfluous.

The information and the detail for the reader who is ready to embrace this cosmic philosophy and, more importantly, act upon it will find all that they wish and need to know within the body of teachings held by The Aetherius Society. My intended purpose is simply to illuminate this path and hopefully bring it more to the fore.

As I stated in the very first chapter of Part I, *The Things I Knew Before I Was Born*, the sleeping princess in the castle has been kissed by the prince and life in the Kingdom of Earth is stirring. I wrote at the time that I did not know of the princess but now, as I write this more than 15 years later, it is evident and even obvious that the princess is the Mother Earth. It is she who is stirring after the great Primary Initiation she received on July 8th, 1964. However, we can extenuate from that that we, too, have been kissed by that same prince in the cosmic opportunities this Initiation provides, for it is those who are now ready to take these concepts on board who are awakening.

George King was that prince, and those who came with him, in their Bravery, were the Cosmic Adepts. They came out of Love, for this all-pervasive energy is "Sacrifice—real sacrifice" as it states in the Second Freedom; and without Love there can be no Service, for Service without Love is work.

That is not why the Adepts came. It was not simply "work." It was a calling: a calling from the Wise Ones who themselves were acting under the Karmic Lords, who equally were compelled by God, and God Is All.

George King never rested on his laurels although he did tend to enjoy what he termed his "cocktail hour." That time of the day before dinner when he would pour himself a drink, either bourbon or Scotch whisky supplemented by 7-Up and ice, to the accompaniment of instrumental music such as the Ventures or the Shadows and when he could at least reflect upon his life's work.

Occasionally, if the mood was right, he might even enjoy a light-hearted mental communication with one of the Adepts, most likely Adept Number Five who had joined him in The Alien Mission. The Adepts were closer to him than brothers. He would have died for anyone of them just as they would have done for him. This was his circle; these were his friends, his people.

Sadly, he had to live with ourselves. For the most part we were all good natured, well-intended and willing, and he loved and appreciated us for that. We had come to help in some of the great cosmic work he had devised or else been tasked to perform. He knew our past just as he knew our future; just as he once famously remarked one morning in Santa Barbara after I had rushed through his living room into the kitchen, "Why are you rushing? There's no rush. There's only God's Time—which is Now—and it's all happened anyway!"

To him, it had all happened anyway. The New Age has been set, and it had been set both by God and by gods. For the most part he had led them, all under the ever-watchful eye of the Master Aetherius.

This is our future. This is The Aetherius Society, and this is George King; a man and a Master I was privileged to know and which I have written about in Part I.

The legacy he has left is for all of us. It is literally "A Cosmic Scripture for the New World."

It is a world to be built by all who are ready to stand beside the Awakening Princess in the Kingdom of Earth and bring about this transformation.

I hope you will join us in this Glorious Quest.

Meanwhile, if there is anything else you wish to know and I am alive, please ask me. And if I am dead, still ask me. You never know, I may be listening and even answer.

P.E.N.
December 20th, 2022
Hollywood, California, USA
www.sedimentofmysoul.com

Epilogue

In the writing of the latter chapters of Part II, I found myself on a few occasions writing in the middle of the night. I could not sleep and was thinking about the book and what it meant both to write it and to share this story with the world.

On one such night I returned to bed just before 5:30 a.m. and began an imaginary conversation with my Master. I told him about the book as if he did not already know. I think, in fact, he knew I would write it and that I needed to.

It was an enjoyable exchange and then he asked me out of interest what I was calling the book. Naturally, I replied, "Maya Mire." He thought about that for a moment and then exclaimed with a laugh: "My oh My!"

It was a jovial moment and, in a way, I'd like to think an endorsement. It was also very reminiscent of so many other conversations I was privileged to have had with him in the final years of his life, most especially in his bedroom as I was putting him to bed.

The Master is missed but he can still be found by all of us, if we want to; and if we look for him in the right places, not least our own heart.

Timeline of Events

January 23, 1919	George King born in Shropshire, England
May 8, 1954	First contact by the Master Aetherius
January 29, 1955	First public Cosmic Transmission in Caxton Hall, London
May 28, 1955	The first known Spiritual Push with Satellite No. 3
August 2, 1955	Founding of The Aetherius Society in London
July 23, 1958	The Start of Operation Starlight on Holdstone Down
July–October, 1958	The Twelve Blessings are given by the Master Jesus
January 9, 1959	The charging of Carnedd Llywelyn in Operation Starlight
April 11, 1959	The Battle on Carnedd Llywelyn
May 21, 1959	George King appears on BBC *Lifeline*
June 6, 1959	George King sails for the USA
July 11/12, 1959	George King meets Iréne and Monique Noppe in Los Angeles
November 22, 1960	The Incorporation of The Aetherius Society in the USA
February–March, 1961	The Nine Freedoms are given by Mars Sector 6
August 23, 1961	The Completion of Operation Starlight on Le Nid d'Aigle
July 11, 1963	The Start of Operation Bluewater
July 8, 1964	The Primary Initiation of Earth
November 29, 1964	The Completion of Operation Bluewater

May 30, 1965	The Start of The Alien Mission
October 26, 1965	The Eviction of The Alien
January 22, 1966	The End of The Alien Mission
February 13, 1966	A Master from Gotha visits George King in Los Angeles
March 29, 1966	The Start of The Gotha Mission
September 24, 1966	Phase One of Operation Sunbeam—still continuing
March 24, 1967	The End of The Gotha Mission
October 26, 1967	The Start of Operation Karmalight
February 24, 1969	The End of Operation Karmalight
June 30, 1973	The Start of Operation Prayer Power—still continuing
March 5, 1980	The Start of Operation Space Magic—still continuing
September 11, 1981	The Start of The Saturn Mission—still continuing
November 11, 1990	The Start of Operation Earth Light—still continuing
March 18, 1993	The Start of Operation Power Light
May 6, 1996	The End of Operation Power Light
July 12, 1997	The passing of George King in Santa Barbara, California

6TH
BOOKS

ALL THINGS PARANORMAL

Investigations, explanations and deliberations on the paranormal, supernatural, explainable or unexplainable. 6th Books seeks to give answers while nourishing the soul: whether making use of the scientific model or anecdotal and fun, but always beautifully written.

Titles cover everything within parapsychology: how to, lifestyles, alternative medicine, beliefs, myths and theories.

If you have enjoyed this book, why not tell other readers by posting a review on your preferred book site?

Spirit Release
Sue Allen
A guide to psychic attack, curses, witchcraft, spirit attachment, possession, soul retrieval, haunting, deliverance, exorcism and more, as taught at the College of Psychic Studies.
Paperback: 978-1-84694-033-0 ebook: 978-1-84694-651-6

Advanced Psychic Development
Becky Walsh
Learn how to practise as a professional, contemporary spiritual medium.
Paperback: 978-1-84694-062-0 ebook: 978-1-78099-941-8

Where After
Mariel Forde Clarke
A journey that will compel readers to view life after death in a completely different way.
Paperback: 978-1-78904-617-5 ebook: 978-1-78904-618-2

Poltergeist! A New Investigation into Destructive Haunting
John Fraser
Is the Poltergeist "syndrome" the only type of paranormal phenomena that can really be proven?
Paperback: 978-1-78904-397-6 ebook: 978-1-78904-398-3

A Little Bigfoot: On the Hunt in Sumatra
Pat Spain
Pat Spain lost a layer of skin, pulled leeches off his nether
regions, and was violated by an Orangutan for this book.
Paperback: 978-1-78904-605-2 ebook: 978-1-78904-606-9

Astral Projection Made Easy
and overcoming the fear of death
Stephanie June Sorrell
From the popular Made Easy series, Astral Projection
Made Easy helps to eliminate the fear of death through
discussion of life beyond the physical body.
Paperback: 978-1-84694-611-0 ebook: 978-1-78099-225-9

Haunted: Horror of Haverfordwest
G.L. Davies
Blissful beginnings for a young couple turn into a nightmare
after purchasing their dream home in Wales in 1989.
Paperback: 978-1-78535-843-2 ebook: 978-1-78535-844-9

Readers of ebooks can buy or view any of these bestsellers by clicking on the live link in the title. Most titles are published in paperback and as an ebook. Paperbacks are available in traditional bookshops. Both print and ebook formats are available online.

Find more titles and sign up to our readers' newsletter at **www.6th-books.com**

Join the 6th books Facebook group at **6th Books The world of the Paranormal**